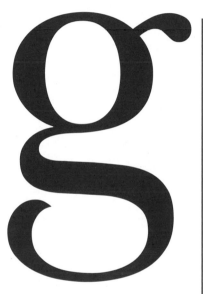

ASA QUESTION TYPES

Antonyms, Sentence Completions, Analogies

GRE Preparation Guide

Knowing the words isn't enough to master the GRE's vocab questions. The ASA guide provides test-takers with effective procedures to avoid common traps. Delving deeply into each of the three ASA question types, the guide provides essential solution processes, plus numerous exercises to hone skills.

ASA: Antonyms, Sentence Completions, Analogies GRE Preparation Guide, First Edition

10-digit International Standard Book Number: 1-935707-09-4
13-digit International Standard Book Number: 978-1-935707-09-7

8 GUIDE INSTRUCTIONAL SERIES

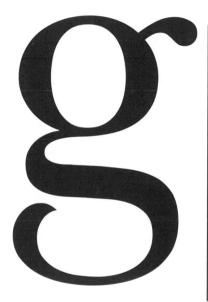

Math GRE Preparation Guides

Algebra

(ISBN: 978-1-935707-02-8)

Fractions, Decimals, & Percents

(ISBN: 978-1-935707-03-5)

Geometry

(ISBN: 978-1-935707-04-2)

Number Properties

(ISBN: 978-1-935707-05-9)

Word Translations

(ISBN: 978-1-935707-06-6)

Quantitative Comparisons & Data Interpretation

(ISBN: 978-1-935707-07-3)

Verbal GRE Preparation Guides

Reading Comprehension & Essays

(ISBN: 978-1-935707-08-0)

Antonyms, Sentence Completion, Analogies

(ISBN: 978-1-935707-09-7)

*Manhattan*GRE

September 1st, 2010

Dear Student,

Thank you for picking up one of the Manhattan GRE Strategy Guides—we hope that it refreshes your memory of some of the reading skills and SAT words that you haven't used in years. Maybe it will even teach you a new thing or two.

As with most accomplishments, there were many people involved in the book that you're holding. First and foremost is Zeke Vanderhoek, the founder of MG Prep. Zeke was a lone tutor in New York when he started the Company in 2000. Now, ten years later, the Company has Instructors and offices nationwide and contributes to the studies and successes of thousands of students each year.

Our Manhattan GRE Strategy Guides are based on the continuing experiences of our Instructors and our students. On the Company side, we are indebted to many of our Instructors, including but not limited to Jen Dziura, Stacey Koprince, David Mahler, Chris Ryan, Michael Schwartz, and Tommy Wallach, all of whom either wrote or edited the books to their present form. Dan McNaney and Cathy Huang provided their formatting expertise to make the books as user-friendly as possible. Last, many people, too numerous to list here but no less appreciated, assisted in the development of the online resources that accompany this guide.

At Manhattan GRE, we continually aspire to provide the best Instructors and resources possible. We hope that you'll find our dedication manifest in this book. If you have any comments or questions, please e-mail me at andrew.yang@manhattangre.com. I'll be sure that your comments reach Chris and the rest of the team—and I'll read them too.

Best of luck in preparing for the GRE!

Sincerely,

Andrew Yang
President
Manhattan GRE

HOW TO ACCESS YOUR ONLINE STUDY CENTER

If you…

⊙ **are a registered Manhattan GRE student**

and have received this book as part of your course materials, you have AUTOMATIC access to ALL of our online resources. To access these resources, follow the instructions in the Welcome Guide provided to you at the start of your program. Do NOT follow the instructions below.

⊙ **purchased this book from the Manhattan GRE Online store or at one of our Centers**

1. Go to: http://www.manhattangre.com/studycenter.cfm

2. Log in using the username and password used when your account was set up.

⊙ **purchased this book at a retail location**

1. Go to: http://www.manhattangre.com/access.cfm

2. Log in or create an account.

3. Follow the instructions on the screen.

Your one year of online access begins on the day that you register your book at the above URL.

You only need to register your product ONCE at the above URL. To use your online resources any time AFTER you have completed the registration process, login to the following URL: http://www.manhattangre.com/studycenter.cfm

Please note that online access is non-transferable. This means that only NEW and UNREGISTERED copies of the book will grant you online access. Previously used books will not provide any online resources.

⊙ **purchased an e-book version of this book**

Email a copy of your purchase receipt to books@manhattangre.com to activate your resources.

For any technical issues, email books@manhattangre.com or call 800-576-4628.

Introduction, and How to Use Manhattan GRE's Strategy Guides

We know that you're looking to succeed on the GRE so that you can go to graduate school and do the things you want to do in life.

We also know that you might not have done math since high school, and that you may never have learned words like "adumbrate" or "sangfroid." We know that it's going to take hard work on your part to get a top GRE score, and that's why we've put together the only set of books that will take you from the basics all the way up to the material you need to master for a near-perfect score, or whatever your score goal may be.

How a Computer Adaptive Test Works

On paper-based tests, top scores are achieved by solving a mix of easy and medium questions, with a few hard ones at the end. The GRE is totally different.

The GRE is a computer adaptive test (or "CAT"). That means that the better you do, the harder the material you will see (and the worse you do, the easier the material you will see). Your ultimate score isn't based on how many questions you got right—it's based on "testing into" a high level of difficulty, and then performing well enough to stay at that difficulty level. In other words, you want to see mostly hard questions.

This book was written by a team of test prep professionals, including instructors who have scored perfect 1600s repeatedly on the GRE, and who have taught and tutored literally thousands of students at all levels of performance. We don't just focus on "tricks"—on a test that adapts to your performance, it's important to know the real material being tested.

Speed and Pacing

Most people can sum up the numbers from 1–20, if they have enough time. Most people can also tell you whether 789×791 is bigger than 788×792, if they have enough time. Few people can do these things in the 1–2 minutes per problem allotted on the GRE.

If you've taken a practice test (visit www.manhattangre.com for information about this), you may have had serious trouble finishing the test before time ran out. On the GRE, it is extremely important that you finish every question. (You also may not skip questions or return to any previously answered question). In these books, you'll find ways to do things fast—very fast.

As a reference, here's about how much time you should spend on each problem type on the GRE:

Analogies – **45 seconds**	Antonyms – **30 seconds**
Sentence Correction – **1 minute**	Reading Comprehension – **1.5 minutes**
Problem Solving and Data Interpretation – **2 minutes**	Quantitative Comparison – **1 min 15 seconds**

Of course, no one can time each question this precisely while taking the actual test—instead, you will see a timer on the screen that counts down (from 30 minutes on Verbal, and from 45 minutes on Quant), and you must keep an eye on that clock and manage time as you go. Manhattan GRE's strategies will help you solve questions extremely efficiently.

How to Use These Materials

Manhattan GRE's materials are comprehensive. But keep in mind that, depending on your score goal, it may not be necessary to "get" absolutely everything. Grad schools only see your overall Quantitative, Verbal, and Writing scores—they don't see exactly which strengths and weaknesses went into creating those scores.

You may be enrolled in one of our courses, in which case you already have a syllabus telling you in what order you should approach the books. But if you bought this book online or at a bookstore, feel free to approach the books—and even the chapters within the books—in whatever order works best for you. *For the most part, the books, and the chapters within them, are independent; you don't have to master one section before moving on to the next.* So if you're having a hard time with something in particular, you can make a note to come back to it later and move on to another section. Similarly, it may not be necessary to solve every single practice problem for every section. As you go through the material, continually assess whether you understand and can apply the principles in each individual section and chapter. The best way to do this is to solve the Check Your Skills and Practice Problems throughout. If you're confident you have a concept or method down, feel free to move on. If you struggle with something, make note of it for further review. Stay active in your learning and oriented toward the test—it's easy to read something and think you understand it, only to have trouble applying it in the 1–2 minutes you have to solve a problem.

Study Skills

As you're studying for the GRE, try to integrate your learning into your everyday life. For example, vocabulary is a big part of the GRE, as well as something you just can't "cram" for—you're going to want to do at least a little bit of vocab every day. So, try to learn and internalize a little bit at a time, switching up topics often to help keep things interesting.

Keep in mind that, while many of your study materials are on paper (including ETS's most recent source of official GRE questions, *Practicing to Take the GRE General Test 10th Edition*), your exam will be administered on a computer. The testing center will provide you with pencils and a booklet of bound, light-blue paper. If you run out, you may request a new booklet, but you may only have one at a time. Because this is a computer-based test, you will NOT be able to underline portions of reading passages, write on diagrams of geometry figures, or otherwise physically mark up problems. So get used to this now. Solve the problems in these books on scratch paper. (Each of our books talks specifically about what to write down for different problem types).

Again, as you study stay focused on the test-day experience. As you progress, work on timed drills and sets of questions. Eventually, you should be taking full practice tests (available at www.manhattangre.com) under realistic timed conditions.

Changes to the Exam

Finally, you've probably heard that the GRE is changing in August, 2011. Look in the back of this book for more information about the switch—every one of these GRE books contains additional material for the 2011 GRE, and we'll be constantly updating www.manhattangre.com as new information becomes available. If you're going to take the test before the changeover, it's nothing to worry about.

Diving In

While we love standardized tests, we understand that your goal is really about grad school, and your life beyond that. However, you'll make your way through these books much more easily—and much more pleasantly—if you can stay positive and engaged throughout. Hopefully, the process of studying for the GRE will make your brain a more interesting place to be! Now let's get started!

TABLE OF CONTENTS

HOW TO USE THIS BOOK

Chapter 1 outlines a few common principles for all ASA questions: Antonyms, Sentence Completions, and Analogies. Chapter 2 focuses on best practices for learning vocabulary. The remaining chapters delve into each question type in turn. You should go through the chapters in order.

At the end of the numbered chapters, you'll find an appendix with three components: a Visual Dictionary, a Roots List, and a sneak peek at the new GRE, due to be released in August, 2011.

The following icons are meant to help you navigate the contents of this book.

Process

A step-by-step approach to a question type.

Principles

Essential themes to keep in mind.

Key Questions

Questions to ask yourself as you solve a problem—especially when you get stuck.

Tools

Techniques to use in specific situations.

Traps

Particular ways the GRE tries to trick you.

Word Beasts

Various types of tricky words. We call these Word Beasts because they can bite you like a rabid dog, if you don't watch out.

Exercises

How to make the learning stick. Many exercises are embedded throughout Chapters 2–6.
This symbol also marks Problem Sets at the end of Chapters 2–5.

By the way, you might have wondered why the title of the book is "ASA Types," but the order of chapters is A, A, S. Well, it makes sense from a learning point of view to put Sentence Completion last. But "AAS" is hard to pronounce. ASA is much easier (and safer) to say.

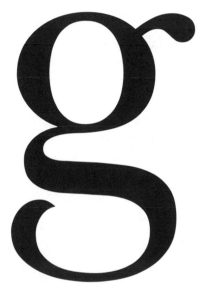

Chapter 1
of
ASA QUESTION TYPES

ASA
QUESTIONS

In This Chapter...

- What Is ASA Again?
- Common Principles for All ASA Questions

What is ASA Again?

Antonyms, Sentence Completions, and Analogies are 3 of the 4 question types on the Verbal section of the GRE.

We group these three types together because they all revolve around your **mastery of vocabulary**—your knowledge of the meanings of English words.

Of course, Reading Comprehension (the fourth type of GRE Verbal problem) also requires you to know the meaning of words. RC passages and questions can be sprinkled with difficult academic vocabulary. However, you are provided with so much context that you can usually figure out the words you don't know. Also, RC questions almost never require you to know the precise meaning of a tricky word.

In contrast, **the ASA types are focused on vocabulary**. The three ASA types provide varying degrees of context, but how well you do on ASA questions is driven by how many relevant hard words you know—and how precisely you know them.

So you need to build your vocabulary in an effective way. That's what we'll discuss in the next chapter.

In the meantime, the vocabulary focus of ASA questions has another major implication for how questions are constructed. Since vocabulary is the critical factor, **the right answer always is tied to the right meanings of the words in the question**.

Likewise, **wrong answers revolve around wrong meanings**, or wrong relationships among those meanings.

This point may seem obvious, but it matters because **meanings are sticky**. Right or wrong, they get lodged in your brain. As a result, for all ASA questions, you need to pay attention to the following principles.

Common Principles for All ASA Questions

⚊ Ignore the answer choices.

You know what is always true about four of the five answer choices?

They're *wrong*. They're *lies*. They are there to distract you. In fact, that is what ETS calls them: "distractors." Like little viruses, they deliver their wrong meanings into your brain when you read them—and once you have read them, you cannot "unread" them. Those wrong meanings are hard to forget.

Don't let the distractors do their job.

Focus only on the stem (everything *but* the choices)—whether that stem consists of just one word (as in Antonyms), two words (as in Analogies), or an entire sentence (as in Sentence Completions).

You might even **literally cover up the answer choices** on the screen, while you work with the stem. This may be the best use of your non-writing hand during the GRE.

SCREEN

Stem: ~~~~~ ⟵

A ~~~~~
B ~~~~~
C ~~~~~   **IGNORE!**
D ~~~~~
E ~~~~~

⫘ **Come up with your own answer and write it down.**

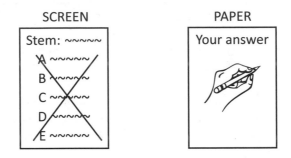

Pretend that the problem is literally <u>fill-in-the-blank</u>, as if you were submitting a write-in vote in an election. Still ignoring the answer choices and using only the question stem, **write down what you think the answer is.**

Don't worry about coming up with the perfect answer. After all, the question is not *actually* fill-in-the-blank. Just aim for a quick approximation.

Only glance first at the answer choices if you really need to. If you need to verify the part of speech, go ahead and glance down. And if you have exhausted all other options, you should work backwards from the answer choices. But the first line of attack is to come up with your own answer and commit to it on paper.

⫘ **Compare to every answer choice and write down your assessment.**

Underneath your own answer (the one you just wrote down), write down A through E vertically on your paper:

```
             PAPER
    ┌──────────────────┐
    │ Your answer      │
    │                  │
    │ A                │
    │ B                │
    │ C                │
    │ D                │
    │ E                │
    └──────────────────┘
```

Now compare your own answer to every answer choice. Next to each letter, put down one of the following four assessments:

      ✓   Good match
      ✗   Bad match *(you might even cross out the letter itself)*
      ~   Sort of match
      ?   Unknown

Do not stop before you've considered all five possibilities. If you find what you think is a good match early, you might find a better match later. Also, an "unknown" answer might turn out to be the right answer, if you can eliminate all the others! In that case, your paper might look like this...

A ✗
B ✗
C ✗
D ?   ← Right answer!
E ✗

If you prefer to cross out the letters themselves, then your paper would look like this instead:

A̶
B̶
C̶
D ?
E̶

III Don't panic when problems get hard.

If you get stuck because you don't know a crucial word, first realize that this is normal. **An adaptive test adjusts until it asks you questions that are hard for you personally**. To get "unstuck" on those hard problems, you'll try a series of techniques that will help you eliminate wrong answers and narrow down the possibilities. Many of these techniques are similar across the ASA types. Likewise, several kinds of traps show up in all three ASA types. Vocabulary is the key to all ASA questions, so you'll use similar methods and see similar traps.

For now, just remember: don't freak out when you encounter tough problems. That's just the test doing its job.

Chapter 2
of
ASA QUESTION TYPES

HOW TO LEARN
VOCABULARY

In This Chapter...

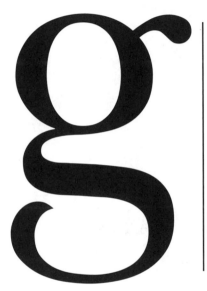

- You Have A Word List...Now What?

- Six Principles To Help You Turn Vocabulary Into Natural English

How to Learn Vocabulary

You Have a Word List...Now What?

There are several good published sources of GRE-appropriate words, often with exercises. Even the Official Guide itself provides an obviously suitable set of words (although not in dictionary order, and without definitions). In fact, you should be extracting vocab words from multiple sources, including texts you encounter in everyday life—books, magazines, newspapers, websites, company documents, etc.

The question is not really how to *find* good GRE words, but **how to *learn* good GRE words**—how to get your brain to own them for good. In the end, the words should no longer be "vocab." They should be natural English for you.

Ⅲ Six Principles To Help You Turn Vocabulary Into Natural English

(1) Focus on the Nuances

Of course, master the primary meaning of the word. But also be sure to **learn the word's other aspects**. Simply by trying to learn more about the word, you make it stick better. Plus, the GRE exploits these nuances, so you need to know them.

Second Meanings

The GRE loves to make use of hidden meanings, even of common words. For instance, *FLAG* usually means "a national banner, a symbol flown as a piece of cloth." But the GRE will make you remember that *FLAG* can also mean "to run down in energy, decrease in vigor or will." *My interest in my job was flagging, but then I got a raise.* When the dictionary gives more than one meaning, learn them all.

When you learn these additional meanings, **include the part of speech**. If you don't remember "parts of speech" from English class, don't worry. The GRE only cares about Nouns, Verbs, and Adjectives.

The tall chatterbox eats a sandwich.

Adj	Noun	Verb	Noun

1)	**Noun**	*chatterbox*	Acts as the subject of a sentence. Often a "person, place, or thing."
		sandwich	Or acts as an object in the sentence.
2)	**Verb**	*eats*	Expresses what the subject *does*. The engine of any sentence.
3)	**Adjective**	*tall*	Describes a noun.
4)	**Other**	*the, a*	Signals that a noun is coming.

Earlier we saw that *FLAG* can be a noun ("banner, symbol") or a verb ("to run down in energy"). The GRE simply adores words that can take on more than just one part of speech. You should adore them too.

Spin & Strength

Some words have **positive spin** or **negative spin**, indicating the speaker's general opinion. For instance, the word *dine* means "eat nice things formally." *Dine* has positive spin. In contrast, *gobble* means "eat greedily" and has negative spin. Your friends dine, but your enemies gobble. *Eat* by itself has **no spin**. *Dine = eat* (pos), while *gobble = eat* (neg). You can envision spin on a kind of number line:

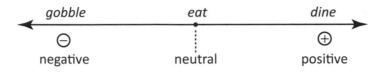

Likewise, some words are stronger than others. *Yearn* is stronger than *want*. I want world peace, but I yearn for french fries. *Yearn = want* (str). You can picture another number line:

	want	YEARN	
	normal	STRONG	

Pay attention to spin and strength. The GRE does.

(2) Give the Word a Network

No word exists in isolation. If you try to learn a word on its own, it won't stick in the network in your head. But if you **provide a variety of links** for the word, you connect it to words and ideas you already know. Let's take an example.

saturnine: gloomy, sluggish (adj)

If you stop there with *saturnine*, you may as well not have begun, because you're not likely to remember this definition. Make the following links as well.

Source—Where does the word come from?

Field—What area of life is the word a part of?

Synonyms & Antonyms—What words mean the same thing or nearly the same thing?
What words mean the opposite or nearly the opposite?

How do you find all this stuff? Easy. Use the Research tool in Microsoft Word. Use Google and Wiktionary. Heck, open up a big old-fashioned dictionary or a thesaurus, which literally means *treasure*. You just might fall in love.

A good network for the word *saturnine* might look like this:

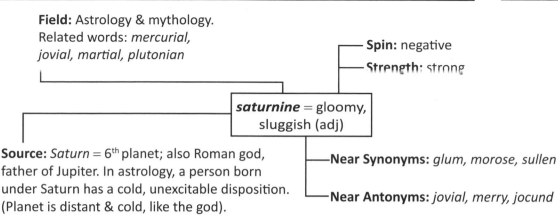

Field: Astrology & mythology.
Related words: *mercurial, jovial, martial, plutonian*

Spin: negative

Strength: strong

saturnine = gloomy, sluggish (adj)

Source: *Saturn* = 6th planet; also Roman god, father of Jupiter. In astrology, a person born under Saturn has a cold, unexcitable disposition. (Planet is distant & cold, like the god).

Near Synonyms: *glum, morose, sullen*

Near Antonyms: *jovial, merry, jocund*

⚏ (3) Use Roots Ahead of Time

Take judicious advantage of roots. There is no doubt that you need to know a good number of Latin and Greek roots to understand modern English academic vocabulary. Many words are easily decomposed into roots and can be understood clearly in terms of those roots.

Other words, as we shall see, are *Root Sharks* on the GRE—they have misleading roots or derivations. During the exam itself, you have to **be very careful when you resort to root analysis to guess an unknown word's meaning**. The GRE loves to use words with surprising meanings.

However, that very aspect of certain words (non-obvious meanings) can help you remember **if you learn a word's story ahead of time.** For instance, the word *desultory* means "lacking in method or purpose; disappointing." That's not so interesting, but if you know that the word comes from a Latin word describing circus riders who *jumped from* horse to horse (*de* = from, *sult* = jump), then you might remember the word *desultory* better.

We have included a targeted Root List in the Appendix. Take a good look through it.

⚏ (4) Attack from All Sides

The key to making a vocab word your own is to use several senses more than once.

You need to hear the word, see it, say it, write it… and eventually use it. These actions need to be frequent, varied, and active. Eventually, the word will become normal English for you.

If nothing else, make up a sentence or a silly story using the word. Even better, put several words into one story. You can always start with *"As I was buying lunch one day, I saw a saturnine fellow and said "Why so glum?"*

⚏ (5) Make a Practical Plan

Keep a jot list. Have a running list on a notebook or your phone so that you have an active source you can add to and look at on the fly.

Make rich flashcards. Cover the back with the information on secondary meanings, spin/strength, source, field, related words, and so on. Make yourself a template such as the one we used for *saturnine*:

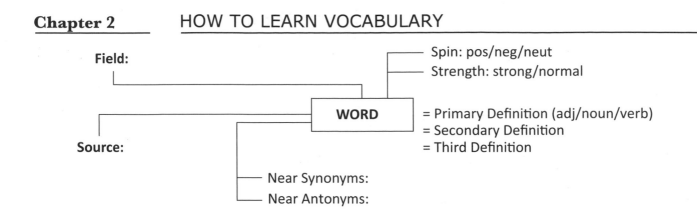

Use these flashcards. Don't just make them and put them in a box somewhere. Revisit them. Deal yourself hands of various sorts. Sort your cards into piles. Force yourself to articulate all the nuances again.

Never be shy about not knowing a word in a conversation. Ask the other person right then what the word means. Make a joke, but learn the word.

Don't be lazy—look it up. There are so many ways to get a dictionary-quality definition instantly that you have no valid excuse for being lame. What else is dictionary.com *there* for?

Use it or lose it. If you don't use your new acquisitions somewhere in your everyday life, then your progress will eventually come undone. Make even just a little use of the words, and you'll own them forever.

Focus on GRE-likely words. Some lists in circulation contain truly archaic, bizarre words that would never show up on the GRE. Avoid wasting time with such lists. True GRE words must be able to appear (even if rarely) in modern, mainstream writing published for a generally educated audience of native English speakers. Be especially wary of "word-a-day" lists, which often venture far past GRE-land into absolutely arcane realms, out of their insatiable hunger for new daily words.

(6) Use Memory Tricks *(optional)*

Some people like to use memory tricks to help them remember words. Other people are less attracted to these sorts of tricks. It's up to you. The tricks can be extremely effective, but **you have to get corny**. In fact, the corniness is what makes the trick work.

Here's what you do. You find a silly phrase that *sounds like* the vocab word. Then you envision a silly little story that connects the sound-alike phrase with the vocab word and its meaning. All three of these elements should be in the story: the vocab word itself, its meaning (at least in context), and the sound-alike phrase.

Put characters and emotions into the silly little story as well. Make something good or bad happen. Picture the event, playing it back at least once clearly in your head. Then you're done.

This process taps into one of the strongest parts of your memory system—your ability to remember *episodes* and events. Decades ago, you might have fallen off your bicycle and scraped your knee. Decades later, you can easily recall the scene. With a memory trick, you can create the same kind of lasting impression of a vocabulary word.

For instance, *desultory*, as we saw, means "lacking purpose or direction." Imagine that we don't know the cool etymology of the word (the riders jumping from horse to horse).

We turn the word into a silly sound-alike phrase and then make up a funny story.

Desultory = de-salt Tori

I imagine that I have to go *desalt Tori* Spelling's ice-covered driveway. Unfortunately, I'm upset about it, so I'm scattering the salt in a very *desultory* way, throwing the crystals here and there *without purpose or direction*. Finally, she stomps outside. "You're fired!" she shouts. Good grief, Tori Spelling just fired me for doing a bad de-salting job.

That's an ignominious ending to the story, but now I'll remember what *desultory* means, forever. And you will too.

Six Principles for Building Vocabulary

(1) Focus on the Nuances

(2) Give the Word a Network

(3) Use Roots Ahead of Time

(4) Attack from All Sides

(5) Make A Practical Plan

(6) Use Memory Tricks *(optional)*

Exercise 2.1   Learn Ten Hard GRE Words

Here are ten hard words that have shown up frequently on past GREs.

amalgamate	diatribe	effrontery	inchoate	precipitate
aver	disabuse	enervate	obdurate	rarefy

A. First, look up each word in a dictionary and fill out a mock flashcard as completely as you can, following this template:

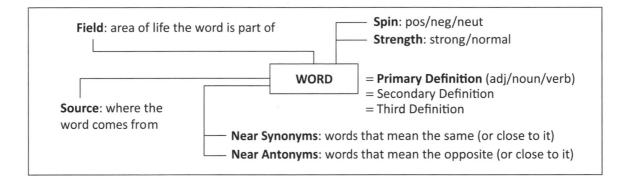

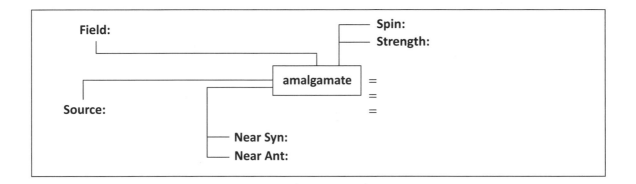

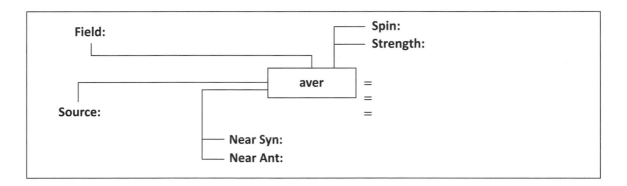

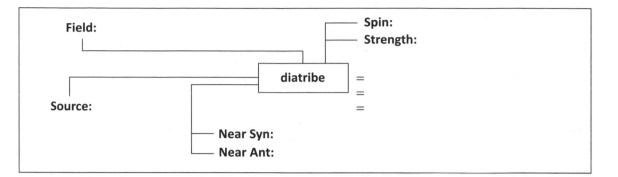

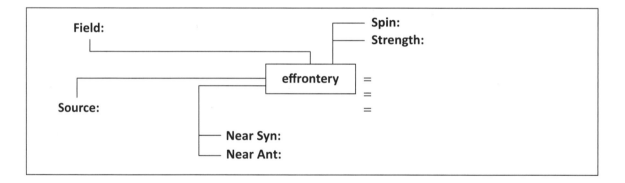

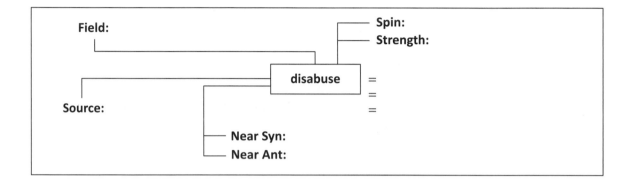

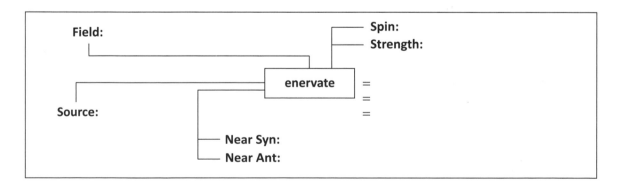

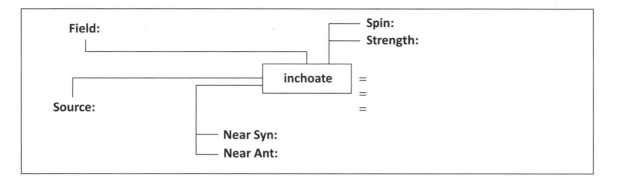

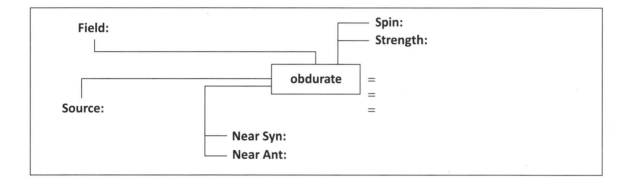

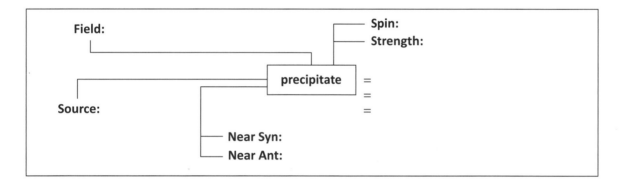

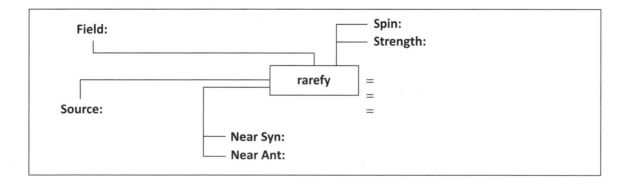

B. To help you *attack these words from all sides*, write a silly story using all ten words in context. Feel free to use the starter "*As I was buying lunch one day…*" Change the form of the words slightly if necessary. Underline each vocab word.

amalgamate	diatribe	effrontery	inchoate	precipitate
aver	disabuse	enervate	obdurate	rarefy

C. As an optional exercise, try the memory trick. For each word, find a silly sound-alike phrase. Then create a silly story that involves the real word, its real meaning, and the sound-alike.

2.1 Solutions   Learn Ten Hard GRE Words

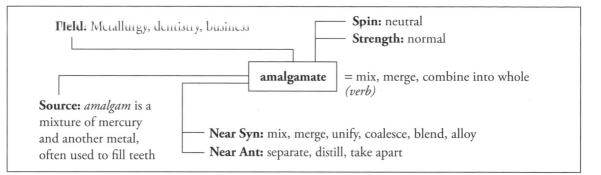

Field: Metallurgy, dentistry, business

Spin: neutral
Strength: normal

amalgamate = mix, merge, combine into whole *(verb)*

Source: *amalgam* is a mixture of mercury and another metal, often used to fill teeth

Near Syn: mix, merge, unify, coalesce, blend, alloy
Near Ant: separate, distill, take apart

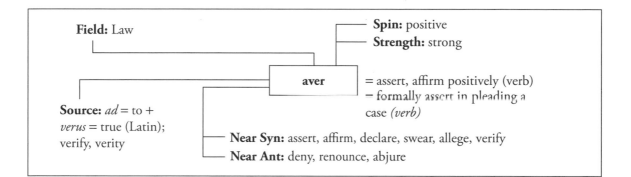

Field: Law

Spin: positive
Strength: strong

aver = assert, affirm positively *(verb)*
— formally assert in pleading a case *(verb)*

Source: *ad* = to + *verus* = true (Latin); verify, verity

Near Syn: assert, affirm, declare, swear, allege, verify
Near Ant: deny, renounce, abjure

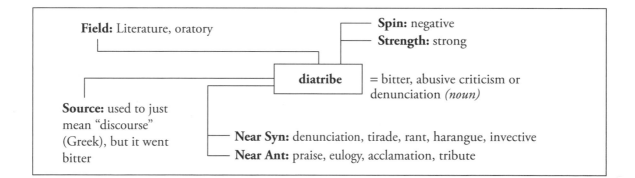

Field: Literature, oratory

Spin: negative
Strength: strong

diatribe = bitter, abusive criticism or denunciation *(noun)*

Source: used to just mean "discourse" (Greek), but it went bitter

Near Syn: denunciation, tirade, rant, harangue, invective
Near Ant: praise, eulogy, acclamation, tribute

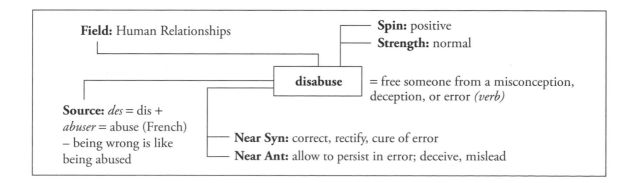

Field: Human Relationships

Spin: positive
Strength: normal

disabuse = free someone from a misconception, deception, or error *(verb)*

Source: *des* = dis + *abuser* = abuse (French) — being wrong is like being abused

Near Syn: correct, rectify, cure of error
Near Ant: allow to persist in error; deceive, mislead

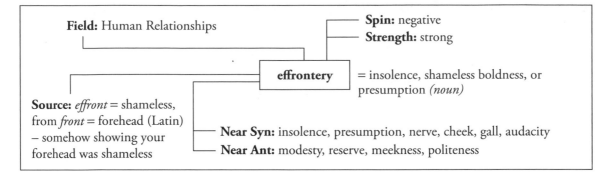

Field: Human Relationships

Spin: negative
Strength: strong

effrontery = insolence, shameless boldness, or presumption *(noun)*

Source: *effront* = shameless, from *front* = forehead (Latin) – somehow showing your forehead was shameless

Near Syn: insolence, presumption, nerve, cheek, gall, audacity
Near Ant: modesty, reserve, meekness, politeness

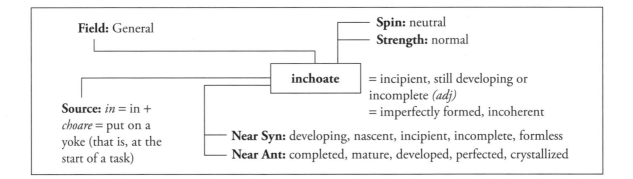

Field: General

Spin: negative
Strength: normal

enervate = weaken, sap the strength of *(verb)*

Source: *e* = out + *nervus* = sinew, nerve, so enervate = take the sinews out

Near Syn: weaken, drain, sap
Near Ant: invigorate, energize, empower

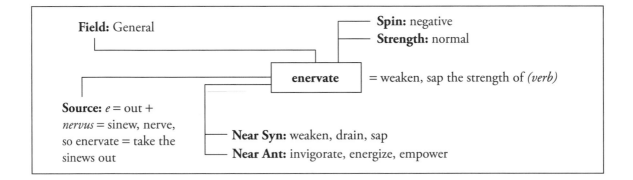

Field: General

Spin: neutral
Strength: normal

inchoate = incipient, still developing or incomplete *(adj)*
= imperfectly formed, incoherent

Source: *in* = in + *choare* = put on a yoke (that is, at the start of a task)

Near Syn: developing, nascent, incipient, incomplete, formless
Near Ant: completed, mature, developed, perfected, crystallized

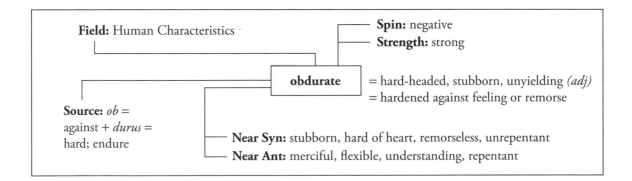

Field: Human Characteristics

Spin: negative
Strength: strong

obdurate = hard-headed, stubborn, unyielding *(adj)*
= hardened against feeling or remorse

Source: *ob* = against + *durus* = hard; endure

Near Syn: stubborn, hard of heart, remorseless, unrepentant
Near Ant: merciful, flexible, understanding, repentant

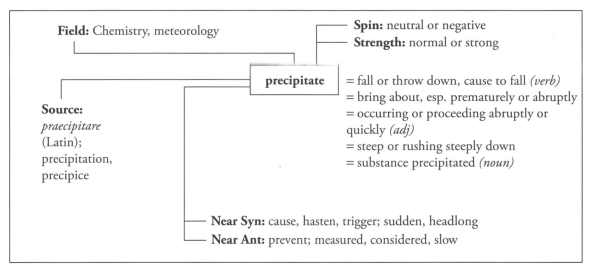

Field: Chemistry, meteorology

Spin: neutral or negative
Strength: normal or strong

precipitate

= fall or throw down, cause to fall *(verb)*
= bring about, esp. prematurely or abruptly
= occurring or proceeding abruptly or quickly *(adj)*
= steep or rushing steeply down
= substance precipitated *(noun)*

Source:
praecipitare
(Latin);
precipitation,
precipice

Near Syn: cause, hasten, trigger; sudden, headlong
Near Ant: prevent; measured, considered, slow

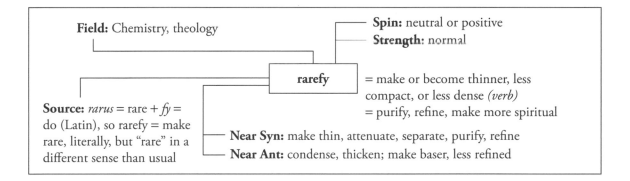

Field: Chemistry, theology

Spin: neutral or positive
Strength: normal

rarefy

= make or become thinner, less compact, or less dense *(verb)*
= purify, refine, make more spiritual

Source: *rarus* = rare + *fy* = do (Latin), so rarefy = make rare, literally, but "rare" in a different sense than usual

Near Syn: make thin, attenuate, separate, purify, refine
Near Ant: condense, thicken; make baser, less refined

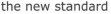

B. A story involving all ten words

As I was buying lunch one day, I overheard a vicious <u>diatribe</u> that subsequently <u>precipitated</u> an arrest. The customer behind me <u>averred</u> that she had ordered a plain bologna sandwich, but the sandwich maker <u>obdurately</u> insisted otherwise. "Let me <u>disabuse</u> you of your mistaken thinking and respond to your <u>effrontery</u>," the sandwich man shouted. "I am a true genius; my sandwiches are perfect <u>amalgamations</u> of bread, cheese, and meat sliced so thinly as to be <u>rarefied</u> into gossamer sheets. In other words, I simply do not make 'plain bologna' sandwiches. Your casual contempt <u>enervates</u> my soul and saps my will to create such masterpieces." He continued in this vein until the cops came and took him away. Fortunately, he had already made my tuna melt, the first bite of which crystallized my previously <u>inchoate</u> thoughts about the dignity of all occupations: this sandwich maker was indeed a Michelangelo.

C. Sound-alike stories

Remember, these stories are meant to be *very* silly. In the brain, this equation holds true: silly = memorable.

amalgamate (to blend into a whole)

> An unwanted suitor was pursuing Wanda McFonda as she was shopping in a Moscow department store. The suitor stood outside what he thought was Wanda's dressing room and wailed, "We should <u>amalgamate</u> our lives, Wanda!" Out stepped a different woman, who said, "I'm not Wanda. <u>I'm Olga, mate</u>."

aver (to assert as true, declare)

> Richie McRich was strolling down Fifth Avenue in New York City, wearing a mink stole around his neck. An anti-fur activist approached Richie with a bucket of paint and yelled, "Before I splash paint on you, tell me what you're wearing." Unflappable, Richie said, "I <u>aver</u> that I am wearing <u>a fur</u>."

diatribe (an abusive piece of writing or speech)

> Wanda ordered a Coke Zero at a local deli. The cashier said, "So, are you part of the <u>diet tribe</u>?" "That is completely out of line," shouted Wanda, and she went on an hour-long <u>diatribe</u> about the cashier's improper treatment of customers.

disabuse (to free from error)

> As Richie was exiting the opera house one evening, a robber grabbed him and yelled "Give me all your money!" Politely, Richie replied, "Allow me to <u>disabuse</u> you of your erroneous notion of wealth. I could not possibly give you all my money, since I carry only a tiny fraction of it with me." The robber shouted, "You want to *disabuse* me of something? Just wait for <u>DIS abuse</u>!" and raised his fist. Fortunately, a cop arrived and the robber fled.

effrontery (shameless, insolent language or behavior)

> Wanda went into a salon and asked for eyebrow threading. "I don't know, lady," said the manager, admiring Wanda's bushy brows, which would put Brooke Shields to shame. "You might want to keep your <u>front hairy</u>." "Such <u>effrontery</u>!" shouted Wanda as she stormed out.

enervate (to drain of energy)

Richie was exhausted from counting all his money, so he went to see his acupuncturist. "I feel quite <u>enervated</u>," complained Richie. "No problem," said the acupuncturist, waving a long needle and counting on his fingers. "I'll just go in and turn off <u>nerve 8</u>, and you'll feel invigorated again!"

inchoate (in an early, formless stage)

While visiting Macchu Picchu in Peru, Wanda found herself overwhelmed by mystical feelings. "My <u>inchoate</u> longing for divine grace has solidified – I want to live here among these ruins and channel past lives!" As her indigenous tour guide rolled his eyes and turned away, Wanda cried, "<u>Inca, wait</u>!"

obdurate (stubborn, hard of heart)

Richie loved eating corn on the cob in his penthouse on Fifth Avenue. Typically he threw the cobs onto his balcony, where they formed a growing pyramid. His butler commented, "It seems that Mr. McRich is building a tower of corn scraps above Manhattan. Perhaps I should clean it up?" Richie replied, "Don't touch anything. I'm <u>obdurate</u> about my <u>cob turret</u>."

precipitate (to bring about, or premature & quick)

Wanda was at a bar with her friend Tate when he ordered a shot of Love Canal Bourbon. Worried about the drink's possible toxicity, Wanda said, "Don't take <u>precipitate</u> action or you might <u>precipitate</u> injury to yourself. Just <u>pre-sip it, Tate</u>."

rarefy (to make thinner or more refined)

Richie was with some snooty friends at a restaurant when his steak arrived practically raw. As he dug in with relish, one of his friends said, "Don't you like it a little more cooked?" Richie replied, "Among such <u>rarefied</u> company, I prefer my T-bone <u>rare, if I</u> can help it."

Chapter 3
of
ASA QUESTION TYPES

ANTONYMS

In This Chapter...

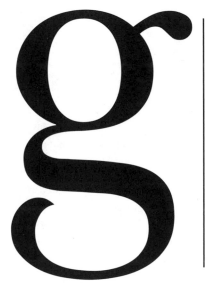

ANTONYMS

Of the three ASA types, Antonyms test your vocabulary knowledge most bluntly, because you are given almost no context. Here is what an Antonyms problem looks like.

XXXXX:
    (A) ~~~~~
    (B) ~~~~~
    (C) ~~~~~
    (D) ~~~~~
    (E) ~~~~~

Your task is to find the choice "most nearly opposite" in meaning to XXXXX, the stem word. This means that you need to find the answer that is closest to a pure antonym of the stem. A pure antonym is best, of course, but you might have to satisfy yourself with a near antonym that does not reflect every last nuance of the stem.

All of the choices represent the same part of speech as the stem. This is the one bit of context that you are given, and it can be crucial.

⌐ Three-Step Process for Antonyms

Let's walk through the process with a basic example.

SINK:
    (A) ship
    (B) fall
    (C) rise
    (D) wash
    (E) mend

1. Read only the stem.

We've said it before, and we'll say it again: the four wrong answer choices are there to distract you.

Your best starting move is to **ignore the answer choices** and focus only on the stem word. Put your non-writing hand over the choices, if you need to prevent your eyes from straying.

In this case, pretend that the question is "What is an antonym for SINK?" and that you have to give a fill-in answer.

SINK is the opposite of _____?

2. Write a simple antonym.

Come up with your own answer: an antonym for the stem. Don't worry about finding the perfect antonym. Go with your gut—and go with it relatively quickly. Feel free to use more than one word or to give a couple of variations.

Be sure to **write your antonym down**. Doing so will only take a second. You'll save mental effort later and reduce the chance of making a mistake.

You know that, as a verb, *SINK* means "move down, often below a surface." The opposite of "move down" is "move up." So our paper might look like this:

> move up
> A
> B
> C
> D
> E

3. Compare to every answer choice.

Here are the choices again:

> (A) ship
> (B) fall
> (C) rise
> (D) wash
> (E) mend

Now compare your made-up antonym (*move up*) to each answer choice. Next to each letter, put one of the following four assessments:

> ✓   Good match
> ✗   Bad match *(again, you might actually cross out the letter itself)*
> ~   Sort of match
> ?   Unknown

You'll almost certainly wind up with the following:

> move up
> A ✗
> B ✗
> C ✓
> D ✗
> E ✗

The correct answer is (C), *rise*.

Let's try a harder example.

FURTIVE:
(A) clandestine
(B) complaisant
(C) forthright
(D) premeditated
(E) serene

1. Read only the stem.

Cover the choices and ask yourself, "What is an antonym for FURTIVE?"

2. Write a simple antonym.

Let's imagine that we know that *FURTIVE* means "secretive." So our paper might look like this:

not secretive
A
B
C
D
E

Remember that you want to write down an *antonym*—that's where the "not" comes from. That's one way to create an antonym (not always the best way, as we'll see later, but in many cases it's fine).

For difficult stems, you might want to write a simpler synonym first. This breaks up a hard task into two easier steps. However, if you take this approach, be sure either to put "not" in front of the synonym or to cross it out as you write a separate antonym.

open

3. Compare to every answer choice.

Here are the choices again:

(A) clandestine
(B) complaisant
(C) forthright
(D) premeditated
(E) serene

Clandestine means "secret," *not* "not secretive," so eliminate that choice. If you don't know the word *complaisant*, give it a question mark. Does *forthright* mean "not secretive"? If you think so, use a check. *Premeditated* means "deliberate, planned in advance." Something that is premeditated may or may not be secret or secretive, so *premediated* is not an antonym. Eliminate this choice. Finally, is *serene* the same as "not secretive"? If you think so, use a check. If you're unsure, use a squiggle.

You may have something that looks like this:

> not secretive
> A ✗
> B ?
> C ✓
> D ✗
> E ~

We now need to determine which is closer to "not secretive": *forthright* or *serene*. Be on the lookout for a word that introduces an unrelated idea. A serene person may be less secretive *or* more secretive than someone else. *Serene* (which means "at peace, calmly happy") introduces a new idea not indicated by the stem word.

In contrast, *forthright* means "frank, direct, straight to the point"—in other words, "not secretive." The correct answer is (C), *forthright*.

Finally, if neither (C) nor (E) had been a suitable match, we should have chosen an unknown word (which in this problem may have been (B) rather than a choice we had definitely eliminated). For the record, *complaisant* means "obliging, inclined to please" and thus is unrelated to *FURTIVE*.

Let's look back at wrong answer choice (A), *clandestine*, which means "secret." This is a near synonym of *FURTIVE*, not at all an antonym and in fact the opposite of what we need.

Think about why the GRE would put in an answer choice that means the exact *opposite* of what we are looking for. The reason is that test-takers often fail to follow a good process. They forget to *reverse* the meaning of *FURTIVE* as they search the answer choices. If you read *FURTIVE*, think "secretive," and then immediately look at the answer choices, *clandestine* leaps out. We are wired to notice similarities.

Thus, the GRE often includes the following kind of trap.

☠ *Synonym Trap*

> = The wrong answer is actually a synonym, or nearly so, of the stem.

> FURTIVE:
> (A) clandestine

We also saw this trap in our first example.

> SINK:
> (B) fall

Do not directly match the stem to the choices. You might pick a synonym instead of the antonym.

The Synonym trap does not have to involve an exact synonym. Quite often, a near synonym is used instead, or a word that shares several aspects of the meaning of the stem without being a true synonym.

Whether the synonym is exact or near, the way to avoid the Synonym Trap is to **write down your own antonym** before looking at the choices. Be sure to reverse the meaning of the stem as you come up with your antonym. Stick to the three-step process, and you'll be in good shape.

How To Write Your Own Antonym

As you practice writing antonyms for stems, keep in mind the following principles.

Ⅲ Pay Attention to Nuances

Antonym problems often rely on subtleties such as the following.

1. Precise meanings

Consider the following problem:

CONVALESCE:
(A) debilitate
...
(E) deteriorate

CONVALESCE means "get better" (generally from an illness). So we are looking for "get worse." *Debilitate* may be related to the idea of illness, but it means "make weaker," not "get worse." On the other hand, *deteriorate* means precisely "get worse." Although *deteriorate* does not necessarily always apply to an illness (as *convalesce* does), it is a much better antonym for *CONVALESCE* than *debilitate*.

2. Secondary meanings and parts of speech

The GRE loves to take advantage of less common meanings and parts of speech that words can take on.

Consider the word *occult*. As a noun, it means "the supernatural": *I studied the occult and similar subjects at Hogwarts.* As an adjective, *occult* can mean "mysterious, hidden": *The professors kept occult materials away from students.* And as a verb, its least common incarnation, *occult* means "hide, conceal": *The professors occulted dangerous materials.* If you see *occult* on the GRE, be sure to consider this last meaning.

3. Words ripped from phrases

In everyday life, we occasionally encounter phrases without knowing the exact meaning of words they contain. For instance, you may have seen or even used the phrase *moral turpitude.* But what, exactly, is *turpitude*? (For the record, it means "depravity, a base state of existence.") The GRE knows that in everyday life, we rarely look up words such as *turpitude* and actively commit them to memory, so our knowledge of these words is fuzzy.

4. Uncommon forms

Sometimes, the GRE presents you with a word that you have more often seen in another form; as a result, you can become confused. For instance, what does *forebode* mean? You might think it is some kind of past tense of *forbid*, but it isn't. The related form you have probably seen is *foreboding*, perhaps in the phrase *a sense of foreboding*. But you might be hard-pressed to define *forebode* precisely. (So you know, *forebode* means "foreshadow, give an omen," often of something bad and as an unspoken feeling.)

As a result, when you are learning vocabulary, you should **always look up the word.** As described in the previous chapter, you need to learn all the aspects of the word, not just the primary definition.

☰ But Don't Be Finicky

At the same time, GRE antonyms are rarely perfect. The instructions are to find the choice "most nearly opposite" the stem—not necessarily the logically purest antonym.

For instance, in the *CONVALESCE* example above, the stem contains the specific idea of "getting better *from an illness*," whereas *deteriorate* does not necessarily mean "get worse as the result of an illness." After all, a house can *deteriorate*. Nevertheless, *deteriorate* is the correct answer, since no other choice means "get worse" in any sense.

Thus, you should **be flexible as you write your antonym**. Eventually, you are going to have to take the best possible match from among just five answer choices, and your ideal antonym might not be there.

☰ Push Past Neutral

Earlier, we used *not* to form an antonym phrase for *FURTIVE*: "not secretive." We can get away with doing so in many cases, but just as often this approach comes up short.

Consider the stem DEMOLISH, which means "utterly destroy, wreck." So, what should be your antonym? "Not demolish"?

The problem is that "not demolish" covers too much possible ground. You could *damage* something (even seriously) but "not demolish" it; you could *leave* it *alone* and "not demolish" it; or you could *mend* it, *rebuild* it, or *establish* it in the first place.

Strong	Weak		Weak	Strong
Bad	Bad	Neutral	Good	Good

← demolish   damage   leave alone   mend   rebuild, establish →

"not demolish" ←————————→

What the GRE wants, however, is an opposite with the same strength. *Demolish* is strong, so the best antonyms would be *rebuild* or *establish*. **Push past neutral** to the other side of the spectrum.

Strong	Weak		Weak	Strong
Bad	Bad	Neutral	Good	Good

[demolish]   damage   leave alone   mend   [rebuild, establish]

GRE Antonyms

Here are two ideas to keep in mind as you push past neutral.

1) **Flip the +/− spin.** Since *demolish* has negative spin, its antonym will have positive spin.

2) **Match the strength.** Since *demolish* is a strong word, its antonym will be a strong word.

You can still use "not" in a pinch, if you can't come up with a different antonym. In fact, this is perfectly fine for words that do not express degree or strength on their own:

Stem	Antonym
mortal	not mortal = immortal
edible	not edible = inedible

Mortal and *edible* simply state whether something (or someone) has a property or not.

mortal = "subject to death"
edible = "able to be eaten"

Mortal and *edible* are like on/off switches. With this kind of word, you can get away with "not" antonyms. Not all words have interesting degrees of strength or of positive/negative spin.

But whenever the stem expresses spin, strength, or both (like *demolish*), be sure to push past neutral. Find an antonym with opposite spin and equal strength.

(By the way, notice that there are at least two ways to form a strong antonym of *demolish*: *rebuild* and *establish*. Both options are perfectly valid, and you would never have to choose between them.)

Exercise 3.1   Write Your Own Antonyms

Write simple antonyms for each of the following. Feel free to use phrases or to put down more than one option. If necessary, first write a simple synonym of the stem. Look up the word first if you have to. There's no shame in that! Use this exercise as an opportunity to learn some great vocab as well.

CONTRADICT:	AUTHENTICITY:	INDUSTRIOUS
BEASTLY:	PREVAIL:	TARNISHED:
INTELLIGIBLE:	RAUCOUS:	MOLLIFY:
PREVARICATE:	HEDONIST:	ENCOMIUM:
HAPLESS:	METAMORPHOSE:	FORTIFY:
SLAKE:	VINDICATE:	FECUND:

Solutions are on the next page.

⊞⊟ 3.1 Solutions   **Write Your Own Antonyms**

CONTRADICT: affirm, agree

AUTHENTICITY: falseness, fakeness

INDUSTRIOUS: lazy

BEASTLY: pleasant, attractive

PREVAIL: fail, lose, be ineffective

TARNISHED: unstained, pure

INTELLIGIBLE: not understandable; incomprehensible

RAUCOUS: peaceful, quiet

MOLLIFY: make upset, infuriate

PREVARICATE: tell the truth

HEDONIST: someone who hates pleasure or loves pain; masochist

ENCOMIUM: expression of condemnation or censure

HAPLESS: lucky

METAMORPHOSE: stay the same

FORTIFY: weaken

SLAKE: leave wanting; exacerbate or make worse

VINDICATE: accuse, call into question, or find guilty

FECUND: barren

Notice that we often have to push past neutral. For instance, *PREVARICATE* means "lie" or "deceive," so our antonym should not simply be "not lie" but "tell the truth."

There may be other valid antonyms as well in each case. If you didn't know the stem, put it on your personal word list and make a flashcard!

What If I Can't Find a Match? Or Even Make an Antonym?

Even if you follow the three-step process and the principles outlined above, you can run into trouble. Remember that this is perfectly normal: the GRE is an adaptive test, so the difficulty will be adjusted until the problems are hard for you.

Maybe none of the answer choices matches the antonym you wrote. Or maybe you can't even write an antonym in the first place, because you don't know the meaning of the stem.

When this happens, you should ask yourself a series of five questions, in order. We will go through each of these questions in detail.

Can't find a match?   Then ask...

⑦ 1. Could the stem be a Double Agent?

Consider the following example, with the choices temporarily hidden.

> NOVEL:
>   (A) ~~~~~
>   (B) ~~~~~
>   (C) ~~~~~
>   (D) ~~~~~
>   (E) ~~~~~

When you saw *novel*, the first thing you probably thought of was "a book of fiction." But now you're stuck. What would be the opposite of a book of fiction? A book of non-fiction? A non-book?

But *novel* has more than one meaning. *Novel* is a Double Agent.

🐾 *Word Beast:*   ***Double Agent***   🎴   *"novel"*

> = Has **two or more meanings**, especially non-obvious meanings.

Another meaning of *novel* is "new, original," as in *a novel idea*. For this meaning, *novel* functions as an **adjective** (describing a noun), rather than as a **noun** ("book of fiction").

Now try the problem with the answer choices revealed.

> NOVEL:
>   (A) frightened
>   (B) hackneyed
>   (C) illiterate
>   (D) artificial
>   (E) impenetrable

Notice that all the answer choices are adjectives! This is very important. The answer choices can guide you to the right meaning, by telling you the part of speech.

To solve the problem, you might write something like this:

old, cliché
A
B
C
D
E

The only possible choice is (B), *hackneyed,* which means "ordinary, over-used, commonplace" (particularly with respect to writing or speech).

The GRE loves Double Agents. We've already mentioned the example of *occult,* which can be a noun (most common), an adjective (less common), and a verb (least common). The GRE particularly favors Double Agents whose various meanings are not or do not seem related. For instance, *list* can mean "a series" (or "to put in a series"), or "to lean" (for instance, *the ship listed to starboard*).

If you think you've spotted a Double Agent…

⚒ Look for Another Meaning

Simply ask yourself what else the word could mean. Here are some ways to find additional meanings.

Glance ahead at the answer choices. For many Double Agents, the secondary meanings have a different part of speech than the primary meaning has. So go ahead and break the rules. Look over the answer choices just long enough to figure out the part of speech. In the case of *NOVEL,* you would have seen that the choices are all adjectives, so the stem must be considered an adjective as well.

Think metaphorically. Additional meanings are often somehow related to the primary meaning. For instance, the primary meaning of *milk* is "a nourishing liquid produced by a mammal for her young." As a verb, then, *milk* can mean "to extract milk" or "to extract something in an exploitative way." This last meaning is a metaphorical extension of the primary meaning of *milk.*

Pronounce the word differently. The noun form and the verb form of a word are sometimes stressed in different places. For instance, the word *console* is CON-sole as a noun (*I was seated at a brand new* **console**) but con-SOLE as a verb (*I wanted to* **console** *the upset caller*).

Likewise, some words ending in –ate are pronounced with the sound of –ATE when they are verbs (*please* **separate** *the bills from the rest of the mail*) but with the sound of –IT when they are adjectives (*the bills are in a* **separate** *pile*). There are other possible changes in pronunciation as well.

As you learn vocabulary, be sure to *flag* any Double Agent as such, in particular if the secondary meanings are not obvious. By the way, *flag* is itself a Double Agent…they're everywhere! The GRE loves this meaning of *flag:* to wane or decrease, especially in energy. That's not what you immediately think of, when you see the word *flag*!

Exercise 3.2   **Expose the Double Agents**

Think of at least 2 meanings for each double agent. The meanings may or may not be related. The part of speech may or may not be the same.

PINE: DEPOSITION: WAFFLE:

PRECIPITATE: STEEP: DELIBERATE:
(remember?)

BENT: BROACH: EXACT:

DIFFUSE: APPROPRIATE: GRATE:

Solutions are on the next page.

⫞ 3.2 Solutions   **Expose the Double Agents** ✄

PINE = type of wood *(noun)*
or = yearn for *(verb)*

DEPOSITION = testimony *(noun)*
or = buildup of deposits *(noun)*
or = removal from office *(noun)*

WAFFLE = ridged pancake *(noun)*
or = be unable to decide *(verb)*

PRECIPITATE = fall *(verb)*
or = cause to happen *(verb)*
or = too quick *(adj)*

STEEP = sharply inclined *(adj)*
or = soak in something *(verb)*

DELIBERATE = thought out *(adj)*
or = discuss thoughtfully *(verb)*

BENT = not straight *(adj)*
or = inclination *(noun)*

BROACH = break through, pierce
(verb) or = bring up, announce *(verb)*

EXACT = precise, correct *(adj)*
or = demand and take *(verb)*

DIFFUSE = spread out *(both adj
and verb, but pronounced differently)*

APPROPRIATE = fitting *(adj)*
or = take away for yourself *(verb)*

GRATE = framework *(noun)*
or = shred *(verb)*
or = annoy *(verb)*

Give this problem a try.

> FREQUENT:
> (A) cease
> (B) count
> (C) occur
> (D) begin
> (E) avoid

The usual meaning of FREQUENT is "happening often" (adjective). Your first inclination was probably to focus on this meaning, and if you were following good process, you wrote down relevant antonyms:

> rare, infrequent
>
> A
> B
> C
> D
> E

Now you should notice that all the answer choices are verbs. Then you would scratch out "rare, infrequent" and determine that as a verb, FREQUENT means "visit often." As a result, your paper might look like this:

> ~~rare, infrequent~~   visit rarely
>
> A
> B
> C
> D
> E

Only *avoid* matches "visit rarely," and so choice (E) is the correct answer.

Now look again at the wrong answer choices: *cease, count, occur, begin.* They are all somehow related to the primary meaning of *FREQUENT* ("happening often") or to the antonyms you wrote down ("rare, infrequent"), although none of them qualify at all as antonyms of the primary meaning. This is a typical trap when the stem is a Double Agent.

☠ *Double Agent Trap*

> = The wrong answer is **tied to the more obvious meaning** of a Double Agent, but it is not an antonym of that more obvious meaning.

The way to avoid the Double Agent trap is to cross out, deliberately and consciously, anything related to the first meaning. If the parts of speech don't match, stop the bus and put a line through that first meaning.

> ~~rare, infrequent~~

Come up with new antonyms for the secondary meaning that's actually relevant to the problem.

> visit rarely

Write those antonyms down, and look for a match.

1. Double Agent?
2. Rare Bird?

Still can't find a match?   *Then ask...*

⑦ 2. Could the stem be a Rare Bird?

Consider the following example, again with choices temporarily hidden.

> SATIABLE:
> (A) ~~~~~
> etc.

The word *SATIABLE* is unusual; you might have never encountered it before as is. But you've probably encountered a more common related word: *INsatiable*, as in the phrase *insatiable appetite.* This means we've got a Rare Bird.

🐾 **Word Beast:**   ***Rare Bird***   🐦   "satiable"

> = Rarely found on its own or in this exact form.
> = More often found in another form (*insatiable*) and/or in a phrase (*insatiable appetite*).

To continue the avian analogy, we call the more common related form or phrase a Popular Pigeon. After all, pigeons are practically ubiquitous.

🐾 **Word Beast:**   ***Popular Pigeon***   🐦   "insatiable"   "insatiable appetite"

> = The more common form or phrase in which a Rare Bird is found.

We are much more likely to know what the Popular Pigeons mean. So, when you run into a Rare Bird and you don't know exactly what it means, find its Popular Pigeon relatives. Use *them* to figure out the Rare Bird as best you can.

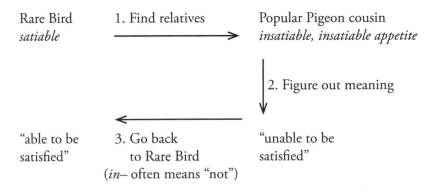

Now that we've guessed that *satiable* means "able to be satisfied," remember that we want the **antonym** of *satiable.* Don't forget this basic twist that's always built into Antonyms. We're back to *insatiable*, in fact, and we can notate:

can't be satisfied

Now take a look at the answer choices.

SATIABLE:
(A) gluttonous
(B) infamous
(C) pompous
(D) dubious
(E) scurrilous

Gluttonous gives us the best match. In fact, *satiable* does mean "able to be satisfied," and the correct answer is (A). (By the way, *scurrilous* means "abusive" or "scandalous." *The critic used shockingly scurrilous language to demean his target.*)

When you run into a Rare Bird and you don't know its dictionary meaning…

Look for Popular Pigeon Cousins

Go ahead & try to figure out the meaning of the Rare Bird from a more common related form or phrase. If you can't immediately think of a Popular Pigeon cousin, try adding or taking away prefixes (such as *in–*) or suffixes. For instance, *forebode* (which we saw earlier) is a Rare Bird on its own; much more often, we encounter its Popular Pigeon cousin *foreboding* (with the suffix *–ing* attached).

Popular Pigeons are often whole phrases. For instance you probably would find *foreboding* in the phrase *a sense of foreboding*, or *insatiable* in the phrase *insatiable appetite* or *insatiable greed*. Often, a Rare Bird doesn't click until you put it in the context of an entire phrase. You may or may not need to change the form of the original word as you put it into the phrase.

Exercise 3.3   Find Popular Pigeons for the Rare Birds

Come up with a more common form, word, and/or phrase. Then try to define the Rare Bird as precisely as you can. Watch out! A couple of these words are also Double Agents.

MARTIAL   FRIVOL

INFAMY   EXTENUATE

TIRADE   OVERWEENING

WAX   PIQUE

TURPITUDE *(remember?)*   CLEMENT

3.3 Solutions   **Find Popular Pigeons for the Rare Birds**

MARTIAL – martial arts, martial law
= having to do with war

FRIVOL – frivolous, frivolity
= behave in a wasteful way

INFAMY – infamous, live in infamy
= public disgrace, shameful acts

EXTENUATE – extenuating circumstances
= lessen seriousness by excuses

TIRADE – go on a tirade
= rant, outburst of denunciation

OVERWEENING – overweening pride
= arrogant, extreme

WAX – wax and wane; wax eloquent
= increase; become
(also a Double Agent)

PIQUE – fit of pique; pique my interest
= bad temper/feeling of resentment, or arouse
(also a Double Agent)

TURPITUDE – moral turpitude
= depravity, base behavior

CLEMENT – plead for clemency; inclement
weather
= merciful, mild

Consider this problem.

> PLASTICITY:
>   (A) artificiality
>   (B) validity
>   (C) inflexibility
>   (D) incongruity
>   (E) insularity

The word *PLASTICITY* is definitely a Rare Bird, with a Popular Pigeon cousin that you can easily identify: *plastic*. Perhaps you interpreted *PLASTICITY* as "the quality of being plastic," and thinking of the usual meanings of *plastic* and wondering which ones could have antonyms (*plastic* itself is a Double Agent), you happened on the meaning "artificial, not real" (e.g., *a plastic smile on his face*). Your paper might have looked like this.

> natural-ness, realness

At this point, you might have mistakenly chosen either (A) *artificiality* or (B) *validity*. Both of these choices are Rare Bird traps. (*Artificiality* is also a Synonym trap.)

☠ *Rare Bird Trap*

> = The Popular Pigeon cousin misleads you in a subtle way about the actual meaning of the Rare Bird. A wrong answer choice is set up to take advantage of the confusion.

It turns out that *PLASTICITY* is really "the quality of being plastic *in the original technical sense*." In that original sense, the word *plastic* means "able to be molded." Once *plastic materials* entered our lives broadly, we started calling them just plain old *plastic* (as a noun), forgetting the technical sense of *plastic*. But *PLASTICITY* retains the original meaning: "ability to be molded."

So we should cross out our original antonyms and write down a better one.

> ~~natural-ness, realness~~   inability to be molded

Comparing to the answer choices, we can now see that *inflexibility* is a very good match. The correct answer is (C).

The suffix *–ity* almost always simply means "the quality of being X." However, as we saw with *PLASTICITY,* little twists of meaning can occur even with such innocuous changes.

Be aware of the possibility that a Rare Bird can mislead you when you figure out its likely meaning from a Popular Pigeon cousin. If you don't know the dictionary definition, take the derived meaning with a grain of salt.

Also notice that in the previous case, neither Rare Bird trap fit the first set of antonyms all that well (in fact, *artificiality* contained a Synonym trap as well), but in haste, you might jump at the connection.

Still can't find a match?   *Then ask...*

1. *Double Agent?*
2. *Rare Bird?*
3. **Guess the Spin?**

⑦ 3. Can I guess the spin of the word?

As we noted earlier, you may have seen the word before. Even if you didn't look it up at the time, you probably picked up something about the word subconsciously—particularly if it has a strong positive or negative spin.

If you think you can guess the spin of the stem word...

✂ Eliminate choices with the same spin

After all, if the stem has a **positive** spin, the antonym must have a **negative** spin, and vice versa.

> PUGNACIOUS:
> (A) rapacious
> (B) impugned
> (C) effervescent
> (D) pacific
> (E) ignominious

If you're not sure what *PUGNACIOUS* means precisely, you might still guess that it has a negative spin. This guess would be correct, in fact. Write down that you are looking for a positive spin (the opposite, of course). Now consider the spin of the answer choices; if necessary, make additional guesses.

> pos
> (A) neg
> (B) neg
> (C) pos
> (D) pos
> (E) neg

Assuming that you assigned the correct spins, you can narrow down the possibilities to (C) and (D). The correct answer is actually (D). *PUGNACIOUS* means "aggressive, ready to fight," whereas *pacific* means "peaceful, conciliatory." (The European explorer Ferdinand Magellan named the *Pacific* Ocean the "peaceful" ocean, probably because it seemed calmer to him than the Atlantic.)

Not every word has a clear positive or negative spin, unfortunately. So this trick won't always work. But you'd be surprised at how often you have a good sense of the spin of a word without knowing much more.

Exercise 3.4   Take Them For A Spin

Try to guess the spin of each of the following words. The choices are positive, negative, and neutral.

ACUMEN: MANDATORY: RESPLENDENT:

OBSTREPEROUS: DISSEMINATE: VITUPERATE:

LACONIC: TOOTHSOME: DISSOLUTE:

INIQUITY: HALCYON: INELUCTABLE:

Solutions are on the next page.

3.4 Solutions   Take Them For A Spin

ACUMEN positive
= mental sharpness

MANDATORY negative
= compulsory, required

RESPLENDENT positive
= dazzling, magnificent

OBSTREPEROUS negative
= boisterous, unruly

DISSEMINATE neutral
= distribute, spread

VITUPERATE negative
= criticize harshly, disparage

LACONIC neutral
= of few words

TOOTHSOME positive
= attractive, delicious

DISSOLUTE negative
= immorally indulgent

INIQUITY negative
= wickedness, injustice

HALCYON positive
= tranquil, untroubled

INELUCTABLE neutral
= impossible to avoid

Of course, this method is not foolproof. Any guess at spin (or at most other aspects of an unknown word) is just that—a guess. Moreover, you could fall into yet another trap.

☠ Spin Trap

= The wrong answer choice *seems* to oppose the stem, according to spin and/or other features, but it is not a true antonym.

If you focus just on the spin of words, then it's easy to blur meanings. Unfortunately, Antonyms questions often revolve around precise definitions. Remember this problem?

CONVALESCE:
(A) debilitate
...
(E) deteriorate

By spin, *CONVALESCE* is positive, while *debilitate* and *deteriorate* are both negative. The meanings are closely related: you might *deteriorate* as a result of a *debilitating* illness. Or you might *convalesce* after you defeat such a *debilitating* illness. Words with well-opposed spins and related meanings allow you to weave these sorts of stories together, in which two concepts seem to be in opposition to each other.

Avoid weaving stories! Make sure that antonyms are opposite *by definition*.

Are *disgusting* and *healthy* antonyms?

No. Perhaps many things that are *disgusting* are not *healthy*. But some medicines may taste bad or even be revolting. The opposite of *disgusting* is "tastes great" or "pleasant to the senses"; the opposite of *healthy* is "unhealthy, damaging to one's body."

Even when you are applying a spin shortcut, be careful. Try to be as precise as you can with the meanings you do know, especially among the answer choices (which often contain easier words).

__Still__ can't find a match?   *Then ask...*

1. Double Agent
2. Rare Bird?
3. Guess the Spin?
4. Use Roots?

⑦ 4. Can I use my knowledge of roots?

Consider the following example, once again with the choices temporarily hidden.

MALEFIC:

(A) ~~~~~

etc.

You have almost certainly never used the word *MALEFIC* in speech, and there's a good chance you've never seen it in a sentence. Moreover, the previous tools don't provide much help. Whether *MALEFIC* is a Double Agent or not, you probably don't know its primary meaning off the top of your head. Also, *MALEFIC* certainly seems like a Rare Bird, but its Popular Pigeon cousins seem rare as well—there's no common phrase or form containing *MALEFIC*. Finally, the spin of *MALEFIC* seems negative, but the question is now whether you can go any further.

Fear not! We have another big tool at our disposal.

🔨 Apply your knowledge of roots.

You have a great list of roots at the end of this book, but you can't bring it into the test. How do you access that knowledge reliably, under pressure?

Split the word up. Make educated guesses: what is the core root? What is the suffix, if any? What is the prefix, if any? Realize that you might have to adjust a letter or two here or there. When you fit the jigsaw puzzle pieces together into a word, the pieces can change slightly.

Write a list of cognates. Cognates are words derived from the same core root. You can remember real words much more easily than abstract roots. Use this list of real roots to determine the meaning of the root.

And don't forget to **consider the prefixes and suffixes as well.**

Let's try out these specific techniques with *MALEFIC*.

MALEFIC = MAL- + -FIC (the E helps glue the roots together)

MAL–   *malformed* = badly formed
        maladjusted = badly adjusted   } MAL = bad, evil
        malevolent = willing bad or evil on people

–FIC   *terrific* = great, fantastic
        pacific = an ocean?   } Harder to figure out. But try a related root…
        horrific = terrible

–FY   *terrify* = inflict terror
        pacify = calm someone down   } FY = do, make, cause = FIC (as an adjective)
        horrify = inflict horror

Putting the word back together, we can now deduce that *MALEFIC* = MAL + FIC = bad + do = evil-doing.

Lo and behold, *malefic* actually means "having an evil or harmful effect."

Now we can solve the problem:

MALEFIC:
(A) condign
(B) benign
(C) feminine
(D) libertine
(E) saturnine

We may not know what all of these words mean, but we probably know that *benign* means "having a good effect." The correct answer is (B). (*Condign* means "appropriate, fitting." *Libertine* means "someone who pursues wanton pleasures." And you know what *saturnine* means!)

Roots are potent. They can unlock a lot of difficult English vocabulary. When you begin to master roots, you might grow dizzy with power.

But with power comes responsibility. Not every word is a simple sum of its roots. In fact, the GRE loves words that are *not* simple sums of their roots.

Because they are so dangerous, we call these tricky words Root Sharks.

Word Beast: Root Shark

= A word that will try to bite you when you analyze its roots.

Root sharks come in several varieties. Here are some of the tricks a Root Shark might play.

1) Disguises the real root.

For example, *malefic* only looks like *male* (as in gender) accidentally. Perhaps there's a deep meaning to that coincidence, but it wouldn't help you on the GRE. *Malefic* might be considered a minor Root Shark, if you think the root is *male*, not *mal*.

2) Has an obscure derivation.

The modern meaning of the word may have diverged unpredictably from that of the root.
The word *sanguine* (= "optimistic, cheerful") comes from *sanguis* (Latin for "blood") in an odd way. In the Middle Ages, people thought that if blood was the dominant fluid in your body, you would have a positive, happy disposition. If you didn't know that story, you could guess correctly that *sanguine* is related to *sangre* or *sang* (Spanish and French for "blood") but have no clue as to the modern meaning of *sanguine*.

Meanings drift. If they didn't, *awful* would still mean *awesome*.

3) Has a misleading prefix.

Prefixes do not always mean what we think. For instance, *in-* and *im-* usually mean "not," but *impassive* does not mean "not passive." In fact, it means "unemotional, expressionless"—remarkably similar to the meaning of "passive" itself!

4) Has misleading cognates.

Two words from the same root can mean radically different things. For instance, *tortuous* and *torturous* both come from the root *tor-* = "twist." But *tortuous* has retained a more literal meaning ("twisting, intricate"), whereas *torturous* means "causing severe pain" (from *torture*, which apparently once meant a specific twisting of the body to inflict suffering).

Even words that aren't normally Root Sharks can become toothy little piranhas in packs—for instance, when the stem and the answer choices have similar prefixes. Try this problem:

> UNDERPIN:
> (A) subsume
> (B) superimpose
> (C) oversee
> (D) undermine
> (E) intercede

UNDERPIN means "support, hold up" ("put pins under"). The *under-* prefix appears to oppose the *super-* and *over-* prefixes in (B) and (C). However, the correct answer is (D) *undermine* = "weaken" ("dig a mine under").

UNDERPIN and *undermine* are antonyms, but they share the same prefix. The various prefixes (*under-*, *sub-*, *super-*, *over-*, *inter-*) of the six words mean "above," "below," or "between." This scattershot of related meanings makes the question confusing.

Often, Root Sharks can be mistaken for more innocuous fish. In fact, this can be precisely what makes the Root Shark so dangerous—the fact that it can be confused with a gentle Minnow.

Word Beast: Minnow

= A simple word or phrase that a Root Shark can be confused with.

We have already seen a few of these pairs.

Root Shark		**Minnow**		**Proper Definition**
malefic	*does not mean*	male	*but rather*	evil-doing
impassive	*does not mean*	not passive	*but rather*	unemotional
apposite	*does not mean*	opposite	*but rather*	appropriate

When you learn Root Sharks, learn them in tandem with both their Minnows and their correct definitions. Use sentences such as these:

Impassive does not mean "not passive" but rather "unemotional."
or
Impassive means "unemotional." Do not confuse it with "not passive."

As you would expect, the GRE loves to set traps based on roots.

☠ *Root Trap*

= Wrong answer that takes advantage of the misleading characteristics of a Root Shark.

Once you are taking the test, the best way around a Root Trap is to be aware of the possibility in the first place. Whenever you use roots to guess the meaning of a word, recognize that you are making a guess. You could be dealing with a Root Shark, whose meaning is not simply discoverable through root analysis.

This also means that you have to do your vocabulary homework up front. Do not abandon your dictionary! Learn precise definitions of difficult words, not hodgepodge approximations based on roots.

Exercise 3.5   **Play Sharks & Minnows**

Using a dictionary, define the following Root Sharks. Also identify a Minnow word or phrase for each Shark.

DECOROUS means _____.   Do not confuse it with _____.

PROSCRIBE means _____.   Do not confuse it with _____.

NOISOME means _____.   Do not confuse it with _____.

SPECIOUS means _____.   Do not confuse it with _____.

RAREFY means _____.   Do not confuse it with _____.

OFFICIOUS means _____.   Do not confuse it with _____.

LIBERTINE means _____.   Do not confuse it with _____.
(remember this one?)

LIMPID means _____.   Do not confuse it with _____.

DISCRETE means _____.   Do not confuse it with _____.

Solutions are on the next page.

3.5 Solutions   **Play Sharks & Minnows**

DECOROUS means ___dignified, seemly___. Do not confuse it with ___decorative___.

PROSCRIBE means ___prohibit, condemn___. Do not confuse it with ___prescribe _or_ "write for"___.

NOISOME means ___offensive (smelling)___. Do not confuse it with ___noisy___.

SPECIOUS means ___false, deceptive___. Do not confuse it with ___special _or_ spacious___.

RAREFY means ___make thin _(technical meaning of rare)____. Do not confuse it with ___make rare (in general)___.

OFFICIOUS means ___meddlesome, bossy___. Do not confuse it with ___official___.

LIBERTINE means ___wantonly indulgent person___. Do not confuse it with ___liberty___.

LIMPID means ___clear, lucid___. Do not confuse it with ___limp___.

DISCRETE means ___separated, distinct___. Do not confuse it with ___discreet (= "tactful, subtle")___.

Now try these follow-on problems. Answers are on the next page.

PROSCRIBE:	OFFICIOUS:	NOISOME:
(A) condemn	(A) colloquial	(A) fulsome
(B) permit	(B) unratified	(B) lissome
(C) retract	(C) permissive	(C) loathsome
(D) transfer	(D) concerned	(D) meddlesome
(E) intercede	(E) tractable	(E) winsome

Follow-On Problem Solutions

PROSCRIBE: OFFICIOUS: NOISOME:
  (B) permit   (C) permissive   (E) winsome

If you recall how we dealt with Rare Birds with unknown definitions, we looked for more common forms or related words. However, we had to be careful. Sometimes the related word with a different suffix or prefix had a twist. *Plasticity* was not simply "the quality of being plastic" in every sense, but rather "the quality of being plastic in the technical sense"—that is, the ability to be molded.

Note the cases in the next exercise. You'll see that prefixes and suffixes can do the unexpected.

Exercise 3.6   Sharks & Minnows with Prefixes & Suffixes

Define the following Root Sharks. Also identify a Minnow word or phrase for each Shark, if you can.

IN- or *IM-* are not always NOT

INVALUABLE means _____, not _____.

IMPASSIVE means _____, not _____.

INSENSIBLE means _____, not _____.

DIS- is not always NOT

DISABUSE means _____, not _____.

-FUL is not always FULL OF

DOLEFUL means _____, not _____.

BALEFUL means _____, not _____.

-IVE is not always CHARACTERIZED BY

RESTIVE means _____, not _____.

-LESS is not always LACKING

ARTLESS means _____, not _____.

HAPLESS means _____, not _____.

3.6 Solutions   Sharks & Minnows with Prefixes & Suffixes

IN- or *IM-* are not always NOT

INVALUABLE means <u>very valuable</u>, not <u>"not valuable"</u>.

IMPASSIVE means <u>unemotional</u>, not <u>"not passive"</u>.

INSENSIBLE means <u>unaware, unresponsive</u>, not <u>"not sensible"</u>.

DIS- is not always NOT

DISABUSE means <u>liberate from false belief</u>, not <u>"liberate from abuse"</u>.

-FUL is not always FULL OF

DOLEFUL means <u>sorrowful, sad</u>, not <u>"full of pineapple"</u>.

BALEFUL means <u>deadly, menacing</u>, not <u>"full of hay bales"</u>.

-IVE is not always CHARACTERIZED BY

RESTIVE means <u>uneasily stirring, impatient</u>, not <u>"characterized by rest"</u>.

-LESS is not always LACKING

ARTLESS means <u>innocent, natural</u>, not <u>"lacking art"</u>.

HAPLESS means <u>unlucky</u>, not <u>"lacking... hap?"</u>.

Now try these follow-on problems. Answers are at the bottom of the page.

STOIC:

  (A) impassive

  (B) passive

  (C) passionate

  (D) sensible

  (E) insensible

RESTIVE:

  (A) resting

  (B) resisting

  (C) restorative

  (D) unrestrained

  (E) unrestricted

INVALUABLE:

  (A) blameless

  (B) feckless

  (C) listless

  (D) priceless

  (E) worthless

The opposite of *STOIC* is *passionate*. The opposite of *RESTRICTIVE* is *resting*, in fact! Finally, the opposite of *INVALUABLE* is *worthless*.

Still can't find a match?   *Then last but not least, ask...*

⑦ 5. Can I work backwards from the choices?

Consider the following problem.

~~~~~~~~~ :

(A) scribe
(B) convict
(C) veteran
(D) detractor
(E) arbiter

When all else fails, you have one more trick up your sleeve. And it's a big one.

Treat each of the answer choices as if it were the stem. That is, find an antonym for the choice and match it to the true stem.

Since the choices are often easier words than the stem, this approach gives you a handhold when the stem is a complete mystery.

Even better, you can often eliminate a couple of choices, because they are Noops.

🐾 *Word Beast:*   *Noop*   🐾

= A word that has **no op**posite (or no good opposite).

Let's look at the sample problem again and work backwards from the choices. Try to make an antonym for each choice. As you do so, make sure that you have determined a uniform part of speech for every choice.

The antonym must be a single word (Antonym stems always are just one word). If you cannot make such an antonym, the choice might be a Noop.

Choice	Possible One-Word Antonym
(A) scribe	
(B) convict	
(C) veteran	
(D) detractor	
(E) arbiter	

When you are ready, take a look at the next page.

Choice	Possible One-Word Antonym
	(all nouns—in fact, nouns describing people)
(A) scribe	A person who *doesn't* write things down? Probably a Noop.
(B) convict	A person *not* convicted of a crime? Probably a Noop.
(C) veteran	Novice
(D) detractor	Supporter
(E) arbiter	A person who *doesn't* exercise judgment for others? Probably a Noop.

Whenever you work backwards from the choices…

🔧 *Eliminate Noops*

Cross out choices with no opposites. We are left with choices (C) and (D). Be ready to pick either one. If you want a bias, pick the choice with a greater number of common antonyms.

In the sample problem, the stem might have been EXPONENT. In a non-mathematical context, *EXPONENT* can mean "an advocate or supporter," so the correct answer would be (D).

As you work directly with the choices, be aware of a final trick that the GRE can pull to confuse you.

☠ *Smoke & Mirrors Trap*

= Many or all of the choices share superficial features. They may even mimic the stem.

Magicians use literal "smoke & mirrors" to disguise their tricks and distract their audience. The GRE does something similar on Antonyms problems. We've seen examples of Smoke & Mirrors already:

(A) glutton**ous**	(A) artificial**ity**	(A) cond**ign**	(A) cease
(B) infam**ous**	(B) valid**ity**	(B) ben**ign**	(B) count
(C) pomp**ous**	(C) **in**flexibil**ity**	(C) femen**ine**	(C) occur
(D) dubi**ous**	(D) **in**congru**ity**	(D) libert**ine**	(D) begin
(E) scurril**ous**	(E) **in**sular**ity**	(E) saturn**ine**	(E) avoid

(last column) } all 5 letters long

These physical and conceptual similarities help the words blend into each other. Patterns observed in published GRE problems include the following:

Beginnings	co– de– ext– in– lack of– process of– be– a person–
Endings	–atc –ation ify –ility –ity –ous/ess
Both or Middle	un–ness in–ility – and –
Words	verb + adverb (*run quickly*) adj + noun (*quick sprint*) number or length of words
Usage	personality descriptions abstract ideas physical properties verbs of motion

Again, **stick to the basic three-step process** whenever you can. Anticipate the answer before looking at the choices. This way, superficial similarities among the choices won't bamboozle you.

Antonyms Recap

⌐⌐ **Three-Step Process**	Ⅲ **Principles for Writing Antonyms**
1. Read only the stem. 2. Write a simple antonym. 3. Compare to each answer choice. ☠ Synonym Trap Wrong answer may be a *synonym* of the stem.	• Pay attention to nuances. • But don't be finicky. • Push past neutral.

If you can't find a match, or even make up an antonym, then ask yourself these questions.
Use the tools and stay clear of the traps!

? **Key Questions**	✗ **Tools**	☠ **Traps**
(1) Could the stem be a Double Agent?	✗ Look for another meaning.	☠ Wrong answer may be related to the more obvious meaning.
(2) Could the stem be a Rare Bird?	✗ Look for Popular Pigeon cousin words or phrases.	☠ Popular Pigeons may mislead you about the Rare Bird's true meaning.
(3) Can I guess the spin?	✗ Eliminate choices with the same spin.	☠ Spin trap: Wrong answer may oppose the stem in some way (such as spin) but is not an antonym.
(4) Can I use roots?	✗ Apply your knowledge of roots.	☠ The stem may be a Root Shark, easy to mix up with Minnows.
(5) Can I work backwards from the choices?	✗ Eliminate Noops (no opposites).	☠ Smoke & Mirrors: Answers are superficially similar.

Problem Set

Do these problems on a separate piece of paper. Remember to follow the three-step process!

1) HALLOW:

   (A) celebrate

   (B) enlighten

   (C) persevere

   (D) anoint

   (E) desecrate

2) INDECOROUS:

   (A) bare

   (B) lavish

   (C) proper

   (D) morose

   (E) lucid

3) MUSHROOM:

   (A) abound

   (B) harrow

   (C) ferment

   (D) ebb

   (E) pinch

4) INSULAR:

   (A) cordial

   (B) polar

   (C) sensible

   (D) fanatical

   (E) worldly

5) STATIC:

   (A) uncharged

   (B) anarchic

   (C) dynamic

   (D) functional

   (E) critical

6) BLOVIATE:

   (A) speak succinctly

   (B) exhale violently

   (C) write pedantically

   (D) succeed effortlessly

   (E) quaff lustily

7) EQUANIMOUS:

   (A) disinclined

   (B) partial

   (C) verbose

   (D) anxious

   (E) languorous

8) EBULLIENT:

   (A) frank

   (B) deadpan

   (C) forgetful

   (D) conciliatory

   (E) forbearing

9) OSSIFY:

   (A) forge agreement

   (B) appease adversaries

   (C) rejoin pieces

   (D) consider alternatives

   (E) ignore obstacles

10) ANALOGOUS:

   (A) ambiguous

   (B) amorphous

   (C) anomalous

   (D) auspicious

   (E) autonomous

11) OBLIGING:

   (A) inchoate

   (B) inconsiderate

   (C) impeccable

   (D) irresponsible

   (E) inveterate

12) COPIOUS:

   (A) sequestered

   (B) seasoned

   (C) squandered

   (D) stinted

   (E) stultified

13) CALUMNIATE

    (A) replace

    (B) vindicate

    (C) enliven

    (D) naturalize

    (E) supervene

14) SALUBRITY

    (A) toxicity

    (B) veracity

    (C) vitality

    (D) cupidity

    (E) temerity

15) GAUCHE

    (A) urbane

    (B) energetic

    (C) keen

    (D) sophomoric

    (E) integral

16) PROLIX

    (A) arboreal

    (B) taciturn

    (C) maledictive

    (D) obdurate

    (E) polemical

17) DISPASSIONATE

    (A) indifferent

    (B) empathetic

    (C) lax

    (D) tangible

    (E) agog

18) ANNEX

    (A) attach disparate parts

    (B) consider additional data

    (C) generate new income

    (D) demolish old buildings

    (E) devolve marginal territory

19) INDELICATE:

    (A) lithe

    (B) tactful

    (C) boorish

    (D) veracious

    (E) pedestrian

20) DESICCATE:

    (A) praise

    (B) air

    (C) inflame

    (D) soak

    (E) injure

21) CONTAMINATED:

    (A) unalloyed

    (B) protracted

    (C) opaque

    (D) factitious

    (E) fabricated

22) PIQUANCY:

    (A) indulgence

    (B) fecundity

    (C) astringency

    (D) salutariness

    (E) insipidness

23) INFELICITY:

    (A) realization

    (B) anxiety

    (C) optimism

    (D) superfluity

    (E) suitability

24) INUNDATION:

    (A) reciprocity

    (B) dearth

    (C) intrigue

    (D) shortcoming

    (E) constancy

25) APOTHEOSIS:

    (A) demonization

    (B) excision

    (C) indictment

    (D) torpidity

    (E) emancipation

26) ENTROPY:

    (A) tribulation

    (B) jubilation

    (C) abomination

    (D) melioration

    (E) machination

27) CATHOLIC:

    (A) ecumenical

    (B) didactic

    (C) parochial

    (D) ascetic

    (E) sybaritic

28) LIMPID

    (A) porous

    (B) inflexible

    (C) roiled

    (D) tranquil

    (E) laconic

29) ARTLESS

    (A) crafty

    (B) indifferent

    (C) facile

    (D) mercurial

    (E) precocious

30) PILLORY

    (A) regret

    (B) engender

    (C) extol

    (D) absolve

    (E) amuse

1) E	2) C	3) D
4) E	5) C	6) A
7) D	8) B	9) D
10) C	11) B	12) D
13) B	14) A	15) A
16) B	17) E	18) E
19) B	20) D	21) A
22) E	23) E	24) B
25) A	26) D	27) C
28) C	29) A	30) C

Double Agents, Rare Birds, Root Sharks, Minnows, and Noops will be labeled. These labels are judgment calls to some extent; be sure to add your own notations. Various traps will also be marked, with the exception of most Smoke & Mirrors disguises.

1) HALLOW = make holy. Rare Bird: *hallowed halls, Halloween.*
Antonym: make unholy, dirty
(A)   celebrate   Rare Bird trap
(B)   enlighten   Rare Bird trap
(C)   persevere
(D)   anoint   Synonym trap
(E)   desecrate = make unholy. **Correct.**

2) INDECOROUS = impolite, undignified. Rare Bird. Popular Pigeon = *decorous*, itself a Root Shark (Minnow = *decorated*).
Antonym: polite, dignified
(A)   bare   Root trap + Synonym trap (*"undecorated"*)
(B)   lavish   Root trap (*"decorated"*)
(C)   proper = polite. **Correct.**
(D)   morose
(E)   lucid

3) MUSHROOM = grow, proliferate. Double Agent. Primary meaning = mostly edible fungus.
Antonym = die or fade away
(A)   abound   Synonym trap (nearly – related concept)
(B)   harrow   Spin trap (*harrow* = break up soil; torment)
(C)   ferment   Synonym trap (nearly – related concept).
(D)   ebb = fade away. **Correct.**
(E)   pinch   Spin trap (*pinch* = constrict)

4) INSULAR = narrow in outlook. Root Shark (Minnow = *insulation* or *island*)
Antonym = broad in outlook
(A)   cordial   Spin trap (*warm & friendly* is not necessarily *narrow in outlook*)
(B)   polar   Root trap (poles vs. island). Likely Noop.
(C)   sensible
(D)   fanatical
(E)   worldly = broad in outlook. **Correct.**

*Manhattan*GRE*Prep

5)   STATIC = unchanging. Double Agent (*static electricity; give someone static*); Root Shark (Minnow = *state*)
Antonym = changing
(A)   uncharged   Double Agent trap (*static electricity*)
(B)   anarchic   Root trap (*state*)
(C)   dynamic = changing. **Correct.**
(D)   functional
(E)   critical   Double Agent trap + Synonym trap (informal meaning of *static* = criticism)

6)   BLOVIATE = speak in a lengthy, self-important way. Difficult word.
Antonym = speak in a brief, understated way
(A)   speak succinctly = speak in a brief way. **Correct.**
(B)   exhale violently   Likely Noop
(C)   write pedantically   Likely Noop
(D)   succeed effortlessly
(E)   quaff lustily   Likely Noop (= *drink quickly and vigorously*)

7)   EQUANIMOUS = even-tempered, calm. Root Shark (*equal + animated*).
Antonym = upset, anxious
(A)   disinclined   Root trap (*animated*)
(B)   partial   Root trap (*equal, equitable*)
(C)   verbose
(D)   anxious = not calm. **Correct.**
(E)   languorous   Root trap (*animated*)

8)   EBULLIENT = enthusiastic, bubbly
Antonym = unenthusiastic, expressionless
(A)   frank   Spin trap (*forthright* is not necessarily *expressionless*)
(B)   deadpan = expressionless. **Correct.**
(C)   forgetful
(D)   conciliatory   Root trap (*bully*)
(E)   forbearing

9)   OSSIFY = harden in one's ways or opinions. Double Agent (*turn into bone*). Root Shark (*oss* = bone)
Antonym = soften in one's ways or opinions
(A)   forge agreement
(B)   appease adversaries
(C)   rejoin pieces   Root trap (seems related to surgery)
(D)   consider alternatives = soften in one's ways. **Correct.**
(E)   ignore obstacles

10)   ANALOGOUS = related, similar. Rare Bird (*analogy*).
Antonym = unrelated, dissimilar
(A)   ambiguous
(B)   amorphous
(C)   anomalous = unrelated. **Correct.**
(D)   auspicious
(E)   autonomous
High degree of Smoke & Mirrors among all answer choices & stem (*a—ous*)

11)   OBLIGING = ready to help or compromise. Perhaps a Root Shark (*obliged*).
Antonym = not ready to help
(A)   inchoate
(B)   inconsiderate = not thoughtful or ready to help. **Correct.**
(C)   impeccable
(D)   irresponsible   Root trap (*obliged*)
(E)   inveterate

12)   COPIOUS = generous in supply
Antonym = restricted in supply
(A)   sequestered
(B)   seasoned
(C)   squandered   Synonym trap (nearly)
(D)   stinted = restricted. **Correct.**
(E)   stultified

13)   CALUMNIATE = slander or falsely accuse
Antonym = free or liberate from accusation, prove blameless
(A)   replace
(B)   vindicate = prove blameless. **Correct.**
(C)   enliven
(D)   naturalize
(E)   supervene   Likely noop

14)   SALUBRITY = health, or state of promoting health.
Antonym = lack of health, or state of damaging health
(A)   toxicity = poison, state of damaging health. **Correct.**
(B)   veracity
(C)   vitality   Synonym trap
(D)   cupidity
(E)   temerity

15)   GAUCHE = lacking manners or social graces
Antonym = having manners or social graces
(A)   urbane = courteous, sophisticated. **Correct**
(B)   energetic
(C)   keen
(D)   sophomoric   Synonym trap (near)
(E)   integral

16)   PROLIX = wordy in speech, long-winded
Antonym = brief in speech
(A)   arboreal   Noop (= *related to trees*)
(B)   taciturn = brief in speech. **Correct.**
(C)   maledictive
(D)   obdurate
(E)   polemical

17)   DISPASSIONATE = objective, calm, not swayed by emotion
Antonym = passionate, eager
(A)   indifferent   Synonym trap (near)
(B)   empathetic   Spin trap (seems opposed to being dispassionate)
(C)   lax
(D)   tangible
(E)   agog = passionate, intensely eager. **Correct.**

18)   ANNEX = incorporate neighboring territory   Double Agent (*added-on building*)
Antonym = get rid of outer territory
(A)   attach disparate parts   Synonym trap (near)
(B)   consider additional data
(C)   generate new income
(D)   demolish old buildings   Double Agent trap
(E)   devolve marginal territory = get rid of outer territory. **Correct.**

19)   INDELICATE = crude, inconsiderate
Antonym = polite, tactful
(A)   lithe
(B)   tactful = tactful. **Correct.**
(C)   boorish   Synonym trap
(D)   veracious
(E)   pedestrian

20)   DESICCATE = dry out (e.g., silica gel packets in shipped boxes are *desiccants*)
Antonym = get wet
(A)   praise   Spin trap (*desiccate* may seem to have negative spin)
(B)   air
(C)   inflame
(D)   soak = get wet. **Correct.**
(E)   injure

21)   CONTAMINATED = polluted
Antonym = unpolluted, uncontaminated
(A)   unalloyed = not adulterated, in original state. **Correct.**
(B)   protracted   Root trap, possibly (*pro* vs. *con*)
(C)   opaque
(D)   factitious
(E)   fabricated

22)   PIQUANCY = spiciness, sharpness of taste, pleasant pungency
Antonym = lack of spicy or sharp taste
(A)   indulgence
(B)   fecundity
(C)   astringency   Synonym trap (sort of; astringent = sharp, acidic in tone)
(D)   salutariness
(E)   insipidness = lack of sharp taste. **Correct.**

23) INFELICITY = inappropriateness Root Shark (doesn't currently mean *unhappiness*); Rare Bird (*felicity* can in fact mean happiness)
Antonym = appropriateness
(A)   realization
(B)   anxiety   Root trap + Synonym trap (near)
(C)   optimism   Root trap or Rare Bird trap (near *happiness*)
(D)   superfluity
(E)   suitability = appropriateness. **Correct.**

24) INUNDATION = flooding or oversupply
Antonym = lack or shortage
(A)   reciprocity
(B)   dearth = lack. **Correct.**
(C)   intrigue   Likely Noop
(D)   shortcoming   Root trap (*shortcoming* does not mean *shortage*)
(E)   constancy

25) APOTHEOSIS = turning someone into a god   Double Agent (*best example* or *level*)
Antonym = turning someone into a demon
(A)   demonization = turning someone into a demon. **Correct.**
(B)   excision
(C)   indictment = accusation (close but not correct)
(D)   torpidity
(E)   emancipation

26) ENTROPY = condition of running down or becoming disorganized
Antonym = condition of becoming more organized or improving
(A)   tribulation   Synonym trap (near) (*hardship*)
(B)   jubilation   Spin trap (positive)
(C)   abomination
(D)   melioration = process of improvement. **Correct.**
(E)   machination   Likely Noop

27) CATHOLIC = universal, all-inclusive   Double Agent (*Catholic* as a proper noun)
Antonym = exclusive, narrow in outlook
(A)   ecumenical   Synonym trap
(B)   didactic   Likely Noop
(C)   parochial = limited in outlook. **Correct.** (May seem like a Double Agent trap: parochial can mean *of a parish*, related to *Catholic* the proper noun)
(D)   ascetic   Double Agent trap + Synonym trap
(E)   sybaritic   Double Agent trap

28) LIMPID = clear (as in liquid)   Root Shark (Minnow = *limp*)
Antonym = murky
(A)   porous
(B)   inflexible   Root trap
(C)   roiled = stirred up, murky. **Correct.**
(D)   tranquil   Synonym trap (near)
(E)   laconic

29)   ARTLESS = natural, without deception, uncontrived   Root Shark (Minnow = *without art*)
Antonym = artificial, deceiving, cunning
(A)   crafty = cunning. **Correct.** May seem like a Root trap (arts & crafts)
(B)   indifferent
(C)   facile
(D)   mercurial   Root trap (artists may have mercurial or quickly changing moods)
(E)   precocious   Root trap (an artist may be precocious, but not necessarily)

30)   PILLORY = ridicule, openly and strongly criticize
Antonym = praise highly
(A)   regret
(B)   engender
(C)   extol = praise highly. **Correct.**
(D)   absolve = free from blame (close but not correct)
(E)   amuse

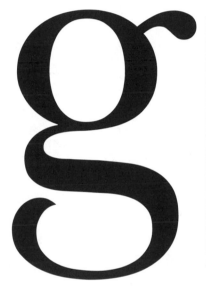

Chapter 4
of
ASA QUESTION TYPES

ANALOGIES

In This Chapter...

ANALOGIES

Analogies problems test your ability to determine the relationship between two words. Here is the skeleton of an Analogies problem.

XXXXX : YYYYY ::
    (A) ~~~ : ~~~
    (B) ~~~ : ~~~
    (C) ~~~ : ~~~
    (D) ~~~ : ~~~
    (E) ~~~ : ~~~

All the words on the left side of the colon (:) have the same part of speech as XXXXX. Likewise, all the words on the right side have the same part of speech as YYYYY. (The two sides may or may not have the same part of speech as each other.)

Your task is to find the choice in which the relationship **most nearly matches** the relationship between XXXXX and YYYYY. In other words, XXXXX is related to YYYYY in the same way (or almost the same way) as the first ~~~ is related to the second ~~~ in the correct answer. To put it simply, you are trying to match the colons, which represent the relationships.

Your task is NOT to match a pair of words to another pair of words. In fact, trying to relate words in the stem directly to words in the choices will often lead you into traps.

Instead, you must first determine the relationship between XXXXX and YYYYY, and then match that relationship to the relationships in the choices. As with Antonyms, your first move should be to examine the stem, ignoring the choices.

⌐ Three-Step Process for Analogies

Let's start with a simple example.

SHELL : TURTLE ::
    (A) root : bush
    (B) stomach : cow
    (C) eyebrow : human
    (D) leaves : tree
    (E) prickles : rose

1. Read only the stem.

Remember: **the four wrong answer choices are there to distract you.**

So concentrate on the stem words only. Pretend that you have to give a fill-in answer to the question "What is the relationship between SHELL and TURTLE?"

2. Write a simple linking sentence.

This sentence should join the two words, expressing the relationship between them. How are *SHELL* and *TURTLE* related to each other?

Immediately you might think of this sentence:

A SHELL is part of a TURTLE.

On your paper, do not rewrite the stem words. All you care about is that word #1 "is part of" word #2. *SHELL* and *TURTLE* are simply the clues to this relationship, which you should now write down, using "1" and "2" to indicate which word goes where. Also put down A through E, vertically.

1 is part of 2.
A
B
C
D
E

3. Compare to each answer choice.

Here are the choices again. One at a time, insert the pair into your link and mark down Good, Bad, Sort Of, or Unknown.

(A)	root : bush	Is a *root* part of a *bush*? Yes.
(B)	stomach : cow	Is a *stomach* part of a *cow*? Yes.
(C)	eyebrow : human	Is an *eyebrow* part of a *human*? Generally yes.
(D)	leaves : tree	Are *leaves* part of a *tree*? Yes.
(E)	prickles : rose	Are *prickles* part of a *rose*? Yes. (Whatever the rock band Poison may say, the right term for the spiky parts of a rose is *prickles*).

So now your paper might look like this, unfortunately.

1 is part of 2.
A ✓
B ✓
C ✓
D ✓
E ✓

This means that we need a *fourth* step in our three-step process. Shampoo bottles tell you to "Lather. Rinse. Repeat." In the case of GRE Analogies, the "Repeat" step is "Refine."

4. Refine the link if necessary, and compare again.

Make the link logically tighter. How is a *SHELL* related to a *TURTLE* more precisely? Think especially of specific use, role, or function.

A SHELL serves as outer protection for a TURTLE.

Put this down on your paper, using 1 and 2, and crossing out the old link.

~~1 is part of 2.~~   1 serves as outer protection for 2.

Now re-compare to the answer choices.

(A)	root : bush	Does a *root* serve as outer protection for a *bush*? Not really.
(B)	stomach : cow	Does a *stomach* serve as outer protection for a *cow*? No.
(C)	eyebrow : human	Does an *eyebrow* serve as outer protection for a *human*? No.
(D)	leaves : tree	Do *leaves* serve as outer protection for a *tree*? No.
(E)	prickles : rose	Do *prickles* serve as outer protection for a *rose*? Yes.

Your paper might look like this:

~~1 is part of 2.~~   1 serves as outer protection for 2.

A ✓   ✗
B ✓   ✗
C ✓   ✗
D ✓   ✗
E ✓   ✓

The correct answer is (E).

A study done by ETS found that high scorers on Analogies do three things better than low scorers:

1) High scorers explicitly compare the relationship in the stem to the relationships within the answer choices.
2) High scorers refine their understanding of the relationship, as necessary.
3) High scorers have reasons for eliminating choices.

In other words, high scorers basically follow the process we've laid out for you above.

Analogies versus Antonyms

As we transition from Antonyms to Analogies, there is good news and bad news.

Good News: On Analogies, **more context is provided for tough vocabulary.**

Bad News: **There is still tough vocabulary!** So we'll see many of our friends again…

Word Beasts such as Double Agents

Rare Birds and their Popular Pigeon cousins

Root Sharks and their related Minnows

In fact, there's even a new Word Beast that doesn't show up much in Antonyms.

Specialists

= specialized words from various fields (such as ships and shipping, in fact)

Specialists almost never have antonyms, but they often have relationships useful in Analogies problems.

As a result, vocabulary is still important on Analogies.

More Good News: **Analogies rely somewhat less on tough vocabulary to cause difficulties.**

More Bad News: **There is a new source of difficulty: the link itself.**

This means that you'll see new kinds of traps as well—traps related to the link.

However, there is one more silver lining.

Even More Good News: **You can often work through these link-related difficulties logically.**

If you don't know a vocabulary word, you already have a series of techniques to guess its meaning, but at the end of the day, you still have to guess. However, link-related difficulties yield more to logical thought.

What does all this mean?

A. You still need to work on your vocabulary.
B. At the same time, good process will make a real difference.

How To Write Good Links

As you attempt to write good links between the stem words, keep in mind the following three principles.

☷ Good Links Could Be in the Dictionary

Avoid writing a nice "story" sentence in which both words fit logically, but nothing existential or necessary is expressed.

Try to define one word in terms of the other. For instance, if the two words are *CHATTERBOX* and *TALK*, then you'll define *CHATTERBOX* in terms of *TALK*: a *chatterbox* is *someone who loves to talk, or who talks a lot*. Ideally, you could add "by definition" to your linking sentence. To emphasize "definition," use an equals sign (=) or a box.

You wouldn't define *TALK* in terms of *CHATTERBOX*. The dictionary definition of *TALK* doesn't have *CHATTERBOX* in it, but the dictionary definition of *CHATTERBOX* has *TALK*, or some variation of *talk*, in it.

Usually, you will be able to define 1 in terms of 2, or 2 in terms of 1. Each way is equally likely to occur.

If the stem is...	... then your link might look like...		
CHATTERBOX : TALK	1 = someone who loves to 2	*or*	1 = someone who does 2 a lot
	1 loves to 2		1 does 2 a lot
	A [1] is someone who loves to _2_		
	A [1] is someone who does _2_ a lot		
	If you are a [1], you love to _2_ or you _2_ a lot		
TALK : CHATTERBOX	2 = someone who loves to 1	*or*	2= someone who does 1 a lot
	2 loves to 1		2 does 1 a lot
	A [2] is someone who loves to _1_		
	A [2] is someone who does _1_ a lot		
	If you are a [2], you love to _1_ or you _1_ a lot		

Always move the word you're defining to the front. This way, your link is more like a definition in the dictionary. Just be sure to mark the link correctly. Write 1 and 2 in the right places. When you are defining 2 in terms of 1, you might use a left-pointing arrow (⟵) to indicate that the link runs in reverse.

Keep your link short and clear. You need to move quickly. Don't worry about incorporating every last nuance in your links. For instance, should you define *CHATTERBOX* as "someone who *loves to talk*" or as "someone who *talks a lot*"? The distinction is logical in theory but unimportant in reality. The answer will be something such as *miser : hoard.* A miser loves to hoard and also hoards a lot.

Find your own style. There is no one way to write links. Short links are fast and effective. Long links can provide more context, be more natural, or mimic dictionary definitions more closely. Experiment, then settle on an approach.

Part of Speech Can Help

As we already mentioned, each side of an Analogies problem has the same part of speech. If you have any question about the part of speech of either stem word, then take a glance at the answer choices.

Three parts of speech are by far the most common: Adjective, Verb, and Noun. Adjectives and Verbs are straightforward. Nouns, however, come in a few varieties worth distinguishing. The first three types of Noun should be familiar.

a. **Person** *chatterbox, miser*

b. **Place** *house, territory*

c. **Thing** *cup, sandwich*

"A Noun is a person, place, or thing" is a mantra many people remember from childhood. However, there are two more important types of Noun.

d.	**Quality**, State, or Feeling	*simplicity*	Derived from the adjective *simple*
		softness	Derived from the adjective *soft*
e.	**Action**, Process, or Result	*evolution*	Derived from the verb *evolve*
		nourishment	Derived from the verb *nourish*

Notice that Quality nouns are usually related to adjectives, while Action nouns are usually related to verbs. Thus, the GRE can recast a single conceptual analogy in a few different ways. Consider the following analogy, together with sample links:

VULNERABLE : INJURE   Something or someone ⎡1⎤ can be __2'ed__
  Adjective   Verb

If you are ⎡1⎤ , I can __2__ you

1 = able to be 2'ed

You can also write many of these links using parts of speech: Adj = able to be Verbed

The advantage of using parts of speech is that the original order in the stem doesn't then matter. Just realize that if both sides have the same part of speech (and they often do), you have to go back to using 1 and 2 to distinguish the stem words.

Because *VULNERABLE* is an Adjective, we can easily make it into a Quality noun: *vulnerability*. Likewise, because *INJURE* is a Verb, we can easily make it into an Action noun: *injury*. As a result, we could encounter a few superficial variations on VULNERABLE: INJURE, as follows.

VULNERABILITY : INJURE   1 = ability to be 2'ed   Quality = ability to be Verbed
  Quality   Verb

VULNERABLE : INJURY   1 = susceptible to 2   Adj = susceptible to Action
  Adjective   Action

VULNERABILITY : INJURY   1 = susceptibility to 2   Quality = susceptibility to Action
  Quality   Action

All these variations have the same essential relationship.

III Link Types Are DUCT Tape   DUCT

You should understand and even anticipate common types of links. Do not try to memorize all the varieties you encounter. These varieties fall into four major themes, captured in the acronym **DUCT**.

D   **Degree** or manner
U   **Use**, function, or purpose
C   **Characteristic** (or lack thereof)
T   **Type**

| WORD 1 | : DUCT Tape | WORD 2 |

For the sake of clarity in the following catalogue, the word to be defined will always be placed in position 1, so that you define 1 in terms of 2. However, you will encounter just as many Analogy problems in which you define 2 in terms of 1.

Likewise, we won't show every possible variation involving Quality nouns (substituting for Adjectives) or Action nouns (substituting for Verbs). These are only cosmetic changes to the link.

Here is the first major theme:

1) Degree or manner   DUCT

One word is a *twist* on the other word, which is more basic. The twist is one of degree (*more* or *less*) or of manner, which can generally be expressed by a well-chosen adverb or adjective.

The part of speech on both sides is often the same, so be ready to use 1 and 2 as labels.

Part of speech	Example	Link
Adj : Adj	OVERJOYED : HAPPY *twist* basic	1 = very 2
	FUSSY : SELECTIVE *twist* basic	1 = excessively 2 = very + negatively
Verb : Verb	INCH : MOVE *twist* basic	1 = slowly 2
	TRESPASS : ENTER *twist* basic	1 = illegally 2

Characterize these differences of degree or manner very carefully. **Spin and strength are always important.** Always take spin and strength distinctions into account. For instance, the two Adjective : Adjective links above are certainly not the same, since *FUSSY* has a negative spin. The GRE loves to exploit these subtleties.

Pure synonyms do occur, but very rarely. Pure antonyms rarely occur as well, because this sort of relationship is already covered by Antonyms problems. However, you may see opposing spins or other oppositions within the stem.

2) Use, function, or purpose   DUCT

The relationship between the two words is goal-oriented.

Part of speech	Example	Link
Verb : Verb	HUNT : CATCH *activity* *goal*	1 = try to 2 *or* goal of 1 = 2
Verb : Thing or Quality	SOOTHE : PAIN *activity* *typical object*	Verb = reduce something like Thing
	LIBERATE : CAPTIVITY	Verb = free someone from Thing or something like Thing
Thing : Thing	BANDAGE : WOUND *subject* *object*	1 = covers and helps heal 2
Thing : Verb	SCISSORS : CUT *subject* *activity*	Thing = tool that Verbs

Be very specific about Use relationships, especially with Things. Vague links such as "1 is used with 2" or "1 is used to do 2" will almost certainly be inadequate.

For instance, you may need to distinguish between a *tool* used in a process (e.g., a *lock* in LOCK : FASTEN) and a *substance* or raw material used in a process (e.g., the *glue* in GLUE : FASTEN). Amazingly, the GRE cares about this distinction!

Likewise, you may have to distinguish between a tool that *helps you do* something (e.g., SHOE : WALK) and a tool that *actually performs* the action itself (e.g., SCISSORS : CUT). *Shoes* help you *walk*, but *scissors* actually do the *cutting*.

For a pair of Things in a Use relationship, the manner, purpose, and outcome of the functional relationship can all matter.

For instance, SCISSORS : PAPER and *saw : wood* both express the specific relationship "1 cuts apart 2." *Keel : water* seems to be similar ("1 cuts through 2"), but the purpose of a *keel* is different (to stabilize the boat it is attached to, not to separate the *water* into two parts). Also, the outcome is different—the *water* doesn't stay apart after it has been cut by a *keel*. So *keel : water* is not a good match for SCISSORS : PAPER, whereas *saw : wood* is a good match. A *saw* cuts apart *wood* "on purpose," so to speak, and the pieces stay separated.

Some Use links represent human use; others reflect a natural function or role. Pay attention to this distinction as well.

3) Characteristic (or lack thereof)   DUCT

A key feature of one word is connected to the other word. In some sense, one word is derived from the other.

Part of speech	Example	Link
Adj : Verb	BUOYANT : FLOAT *derived* basic	Adj. = able to Verb
Verb : Adj	EXPLAIN : CLEAR *derived* basic	Verb = make something Adj
Adj : Thing or Quality	DIM (adj) : LIGHT (noun) *derived* basic	Adj = lacking Thing or Quality
Person : Adj	SAGE : WISE *derived* basic	Person = someone who is Adj
Thing : Thing	SPLINTER : WOOD *derived* basic	1 = thin broken piece of 2

In the last case, one word (SPLINTER) is even physically derived from the other (WOOD).

The examples shown above are not exhaustive. For instance, Adjectives defined in terms of Verbs could match the following templates:

Adj. = able to Verb	BUOYANT : FLOAT
Adj. = not able to Verb	BUOYANT : SINK
Adj. = willing or quick to Verb	AGGRESSIVE : ATTACK

Often, one word expresses a Characteristic of the other word. Almost as often, one word expresses the *lack* of a Characteristic (e.g., DIM : LIGHT or BUOYANT : SINK).

Remember, to determine part of speech for words that can take on various parts of speech (e.g., DIM or LIGHT), glance at the five answer choices. Parts of speech will *never be* labeled as we have done above. And remember, if you're checking for part of speech, don't linger on the answer choices! Just take a glance, identify the part of speech, and go back to the stem.

4) Type   DUCT

Type is similar to and overlaps with Characteristic.

Part of speech	Example	Link
Thing : Thing	TABLE : FURNITURE *member* group	1 = type of 2
Thing : Thing	TYPHOON : STORM *specific* *general*	1 = big, bad type of 2
Thing : Adj or Quality	CLICHÉ (noun) : TRITE *specific* *attribute*	Thing = Adjective type of expression
Adj : Thing	COHERENT : ARGUMENT *category* *general*	An Adjective Thing = one that hangs together well

A possible match for the last link would be *harmonious : music.*

Watch out for pure membership. Be ready to choose this deceptively simple relationship, which seems almost *too* simple. The correct link for TABLE : FURNITURE is simply "A TABLE is a type of FURNITURE." If this were the stem, the right answer could be *knee : joint.* A *knee* is a type of *joint.* Even though no other aspect or feature applies, pure membership is sufficient.

What makes it confusing is that a TABLE and a *knee* don't seem to be similar. This is one reason why it is so dangerous to look for similarities *vertically* among the words.

In contrast, TYPHOON : STORM is more likely asking for you to specify the kind of storm, since those specific characteristics ("big and bad") could be easily applied in another situation having nothing to do with meteorology. For instance, *mob : crowd* would work.

How do you know when the GRE wants the specific type (TYPHOON : STORM) and when it can accept simple membership (TABLE : FURNITURE)? If you can't articulate the specific type easily, in just a couple of words, then you're probably dealing with pure membership. For instance, it would be difficult to see how the specific characteristics of a TABLE that distinguish it from other kinds of FURNITURE (e.g., "has legs and a flat top") could be brought over to other realms.

Moreover, the answer choices will guide you. Be ready to select a choice that only indicates membership in a group.

Now that you've seen all four themes, take a quick glance back over them. Where do you see Thing: Thing? If you have two objects in the stem, there are only a few possible links (because (1) Degree doesn't appear with two objects).

2) Use	1 does something to 2 "on purpose," or vice versa.
3) Characteristic	1 is a part of 2 or is made from 2, or vice versa.
4) Type	1 is a specific type of 2, or vice versa.

Exercise 4.1   Hit the Links with DUCT Tape ⬚DUCT

Define the following links. Use either numbers (1 and 2) or part-of-speech abbreviations. Be ready to define 2 in terms of 1. If you can, classify each link as Degree, Use, Characteristic, or Type.

SCAN (verb) : READ   APPEARANCE : VAIN

COMMENT (verb) : DISPARAGE   MINE (verb) : DIAMOND

TEACH : LEARN   DEITY : DEIFY

READ : ILLEGIBLE   CARRION : MAGGOT

HUNGRY : FOOD   ORGAN : LIVER

MORTAR (noun) : BIND   SPEND : SPENDTHRIFT (noun)

▥ **4.1 Solutions**   **Hit the Links with DUCT Tape** DUCT

SCAN (verb) : READ
Degree | 1 | = do 2 quickly/lightly

COMMENT (verb) : DISPARAGE
Degree | 2 | = do 1 hurtfully, negatively

TEACH : LEARN
Use | 1 | = cause people to do 2

READ : ILLEGIBLE
Characteristic | Adj. | = unable to be Verbed

HUNGRY : FOOD
Characteristic | Adj. | = desiring Thing

MORTAR (noun) : BIND
Use | Noun | = substance that does
                              Verb

APPEARANCE : VAIN
Characteristic | Adj. | = caring too much about Thing

MINE (verb) : DIAMOND
Use | Verb | = extract something such
                              as Thing for use

DEITY : DEIFY
Characteristic | Verb | = turn someone into Thing

CARRION : MAGGOT
Use | 2 | = lives/grows in 1

ORGAN : LIVER
Type | 2 | = type of 1

SPEND : SPENDTHRIFT (noun)
Characteristic | Person | = does 2 excessively

Quirky Links

What if you know the words, but you can't find a dictionary-quality link? Try the following two techniques.

✖ Push more meaning into the link.

Consider this example.   PROCLAIM : PUBLIC

First, figure out which way the definition would go. Would *PROCLAIM* show up in the definition of *PUBLIC*, or would *PUBLIC* show up in the definition of *PROCLAIM*?

PROCLAIM means "to speak in a public way" or "state something publicly."

Now keep everything besides *PUBLIC*. The link is this: | Verb | = **speak** in an Adjective way

The verb *speak* is a key part of the link and must show up in the right answer. For instance, the answer could be *whisper : quiet*, since *whisper* = **speak** in a *quiet* way.

Earlier, we saw several examples in which the link itself contains **substantial** meaning (bolded below). Specific actions or things can show up in certain links. Be ready for this.

SOOTHE : PAIN	| Verb | = **reduce** something like Thing
CLICHÉ (noun) : TRITE	| Thing | = Adjective type of **expression**
COHERENT : ARGUMENT	An Adjective | Thing | = one that **hangs together well**

✖ Define *both* words as versions of a 3ʳᵈ thing.

Look at this example.   COTTAGE : PALACE

Would the dictionary define a *COTTAGE* in terms of a *PALACE*, or vice versa? No. Both are specific types of *houses* or *habitations*. This is the exception to the rule that you can define one word in terms of the other. However, now that you have seen this sort of link, it is easy to recognize and tackle. Just write a slightly longer link, using "version" and "but" to emphasize the contrast.

COTTAGE : PALACE | 1 | = a **small** version of something, but | 2 | = a **big** version of that thing

Don't write the word "house"—just write "something." What matters is the variation: **small** and **big**.

The right answer could be *booklet : tome*. A *booklet* is a **small** version (of a book), but a *tome* is a **big** version (of a book). It doesn't matter that "house" and "book" have no necessary relationship.

Similarly, the link in NIBBLE : WOLF (verb) could be put in the following way.

    | 1 | = (*eat*) **a little at intervals**, but | 2 | = (*eat*) **a lot impulsively**

The correct answer could be *stammer : blurt*. *Stammer* = "speak **a little at intervals**," while *blurt* – "speak **a lot impulsively**." Note that "eat" and "speak" are both unimportant, just as "house" and "book" were.

Quirky Words

As we noted earlier, the GRE makes use of a new Word Beast on Analogies problems: Specialists. 🚢

Get ready for jargon from all walks of life! Specialist words tend to be concrete nouns—that is, nouns that represent very specific physical objects, although there are some specialized verbs pertaining to farming, engineering, and so on.

This may be a special area of difficulty for non-native speakers. Of course, few students taking the GRE have a strong knowledge of sailing, tool usage, and architecture, among other topics from which the following words have been gathered. Learning these words will provide an edge on the GRE.

Learn the meanings of these words as precisely as you can. For instance, simply knowing that an axle is a machine part or that a frigate is a boat won't help with WHEEL : AXLE (a *WHEEL* **rotates around** an *AXLE*) or FRIGATE : WARSHIP (a *FRIGATE* is a **type** of *WARSHIP*). At the same time, you don't need to know everything about each Specialist. All you really need to know about SONNET is that it is a type of poem, not how many lines it has and how the rhymes work. Remember the DUCT links: things will be related by Degree (big or small), Use (function), Charateristic, and Type.

To help you learn these Specialists efficiently, we have compiled a Visual Dictionary of a few hundred words, most of which have appeared on Analogies questions published by the GRE. A few of these questions are asterisked in the Official Guide, meaning that they would not meet the current standards of the GRE. However, the overall use of Specialists has continued strongly through recent exams, so we've kept the relevant words.

The Visual Dictionary is no substitute for a true dictionary. You should look up any unfamiliar words on the list below and use the Visual Dictionary only as a starting point. We start the Visual Dictionary with the GRE's unexplained obsession with ships, then continue with the natural world, farming, and transportation. By the way, you'll need a very basic sense of biological categories: for instance, oaks and pines are types of trees, but a lizard is not a type of frog (nor vice versa). Also, you should know a little about what turns into what (acorns into oaks, tadpoles into frogs). Isn't this fun?

Parts of a Ship   Types of Ships

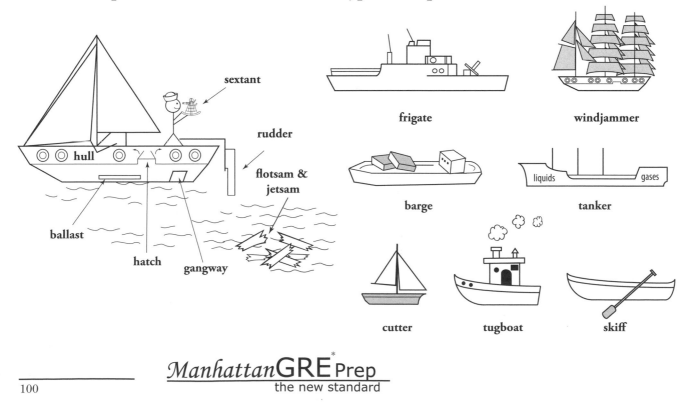

The Natural World, Farming, & Transportation

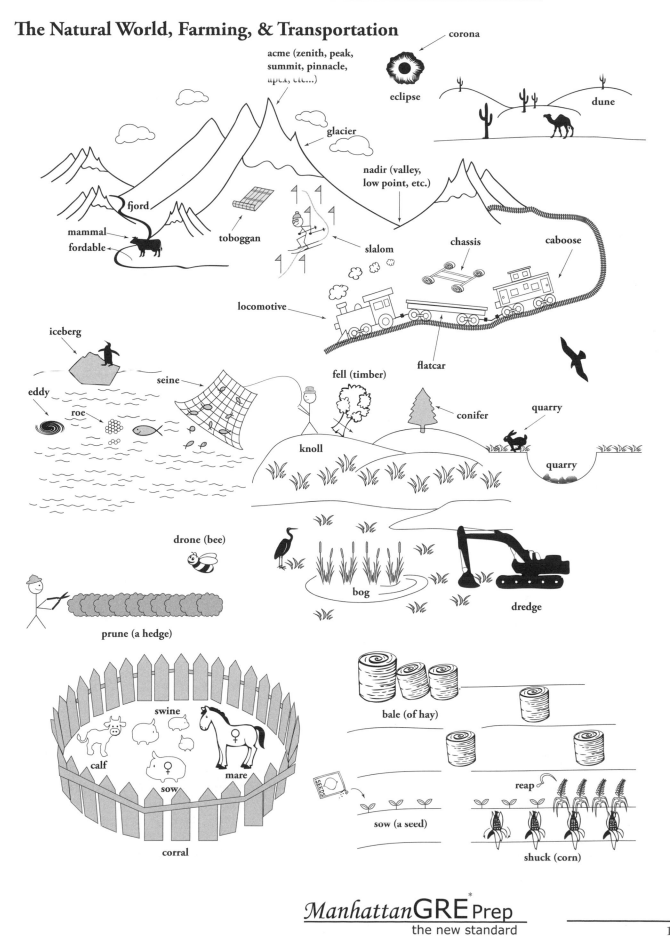

For more pages of the Visual Dictionary, turn to page 139. Do not try to become an expert in each of these areas! Just familiarize yourself gradually with these Specialist words over time, and have a good time sprinkling the jargon into conversation. Eventually, you should be able to recognize and define every word in the Visual Dictionary.

Familiar Techniques & Traps

Whenever we see our old Word Beast friends again, we'll encounter many of the same traps and use the same techniques.

⑦ **Key Questions**	✖ **Tools**	☠ **Traps**
Could the word be a Double Agent?	✖ Look for another meaning.	☠ Wrong answer may be related to the more obvious meaning.
Could the word be a Rare Bird?	✖ Look for Popular Pigeon cousin words or phrases.	☠ Popular Pigeons may mislead you about the Rare Bird's true meaning.
Can I use roots?	✖ Apply your knowledge of roots.	☠ The stem may be a Root Shark, easy to mix up with Minnows.

Consider the following problem.

OBTAIN : MILK ::
  (A) drain : secrete
  (B) measure : prorate
  (C) collect : hoard
  (D) grow : burgeon
  (E) exploit : raise

MILK is a classic Double Agent. **Scan the answer choices to determine the part of speech, if necessary.** Since we see *secrete, prorate*, etc., we know that *MILK* is being used as a Verb. *MILK* still has more than one meaning as a Verb: it can mean "to extract milk from a cow" or "to exploit or extract to someone else's detriment." The latter meaning seems more promising, so we set up a link on our paper.

2 = do 1 negatively/harmfully
A
B
C
D
E

Now we evaluate our choices one at a time. Be sure to put the second word first. *Hoard* can mean "collect in a negative way, to someone else's detriment." The match isn't 100% perfect, but it's very close and also the closest available. The correct answer is (C).

Notice that wrong answer (A) is related to other meanings of *MILK*. This is a classic Double Agent trap.

New Methods—and New Traps (Sort Of)

We have five new methods and several new traps for Analogies. However, you'll see many of the same principles that we discussed for Antonyms.

- -

Like the other ASA types, Analogies take advantage of subtleties. Take a look at this example.

SHEAR : SHEEP ::
(A) shed : snake
(E) shell : shrimp

The three cases contain strong "by definition" links, which are very similar in meaning.

SHEAR : SHEEP	SHEAR a SHEEP = remove its outer layer
	Verb = **remove** the outer layer of something like Thing
shed : snake	a snake sheds = removes its own outer layer
	Thing Verbs = **removes** its own outer layer
shell : shrimp	shell a shrimp = remove its outer layer
	Verb = **remove** the outer layer of something like Thing

The correct answer is (E). But (A) is very close. All that has really been changed is the role of the animal: in the case of SHEAR : SHEEP and *shell : shrimp*, the animals are objects of the verb (you shear a sheep or shell a shrimp), but in the case of *shed : snake,* the animal is the subject of the verb (a snake sheds its own skin). This reversal is very subtle, and under test pressure, you might miss it.

☠ *Reversal Trap*

> = The answer choice is almost right, but one aspect of the meaning has been subtly reversed.

There was another subtle trap on the previous page.

OBTAIN : MILK ::
(D) grow : burgeon

The stem link was this: 2 = do 1 negatively/harmfully. But *burgeon* means "grow *rapidly*," not necessarily harmfully (though it could be). *Grow : burgeon* is a Spin/Strength Trap.

☠ *Spin/Strength Trap*

> = The choice is almost right, but the spin and/or the strength are not quite right.

To avoid both of these traps, apply Method #1:

⚒ 1. Compare the link carefully to the answer choices.

This is part of the basic process (Step #3), but it's worth restating. Watch out for slight differences. They matter.

*Manhattan*GRE*Prep
the new standard

- -

Look again at the truncated SHEAR : SHEEP problem, and say all the words aloud.

SHEAR : SHEEP ::
(A) shed : snake
...
(E) shell : shrimp

You probably noticed that all the words begin with *s-* (five with *sh-*, in fact). They're all short, too, with just one syllable each. If you read this problem aloud a couple of times, it would start to sound like Dr. Seuss (if it doesn't already). Moreover, all the words on the right are animals, and all the words on the left are verbs relating to the removal of an outer layer.

To the GRE, that's a wonderful, confusing effect. The GRE applies this sort of smoke screen quite often.

☠ *Smoke & Mirrors Trap*

> = Many or all of the choices share superficial features. They may even mimic the stem.

Although we ran into this trap on Antonyms, it's even more deadly on Analogies. The reason is that students often do the wrong thing. They just vertically compare words, looking for similarities on the left and similarities on the right.

The GRE knows this, and so it puts in words that are **thematically related** to the stem. It's so easy to fall for this particular variation that we need to give it its own skull and crossbones.

☠ *Theme Trap*

> = The wrong answer choice shares a theme or field with the stem.

This is particularly deadly when the right answer is not thematically related to the stem. Remember, the same definitional link can work between pairs of words in vastly different fields, so this is not only possible, it's desirable from the GRE's point of view. The GRE tries as much as it can to disguise the right answer by putting the words in a distant field.

So, **if you *must* guess randomly, actually avoid the choice thematically related to the stem!**

To avoid Smoke & Mirrors and its deadly variant, the Theme trap…

✎ 2. Ignore vertical similarities or vertical relationships among individual words.

Make sure you are only matching **colons**. Always construct **horizontal** relationships first, then compare those relationships.

- -

What do we do when we work backwards?

Remember that in Antonyms, we could eliminate **Noop** choices—choices that had **No Op**posites?

In Analogies, we can do something very similar. We can eliminate **NO-DEF** choices.

Link Beast: NO-DEF

— Two words that have NO DEFinitional link (such as a fish and a bicycle).

NO-DEF choices are very common. The words may seem to be related, but not in a strict, logically consistent way. Consider the following example, in which the stem and one answer choice are obscured.

> XXXXX : YYYYY ::
> (A) impartial : consideration
> (B) mournful : plea
> (C) lengthy : wait
> (D) heroic : tale
> (E) ~~~~~ : ~~~~~

Does a *consideration* have to be *impartial*? No. It might be, it might not. Likewise, a *plea* does not have to be *mournful*, a *wait* does not have to be *lengthy*, and a *tale* does not have to be *heroic*. All these pairs of words have a "could be" relationship (i.e., a plea could be mournful, a wait could be lengthy). This does not lend itself to a defined relationship. The answer choices are NO-DEF choices, and so we can eliminate them. Without even seeing choice (E), we know it is very likely to be correct.

Whenever you work backwards from the choices…

3. Eliminate NO-DEFs.

Cross out choices that contain no definitional link.

The GRE doesn't pick two words at random for NO-DEFs. It finds a fake relationship.

Fake Relationship Trap for NO-DEFs

= Pair of words related in a non-definitional way.

For example, the words are found together in a **common phrase** (*mournful plea*). Or they have a **thematic connection** (*lengthy* and *wait*), but not a necessary one. Or you can tell a **likely story** (*heroic* and *tale*) that weaves a loose connection between the two words.

Here is the key test.

⑦ Can you define one word in terms of the other?

If you're having trouble defining one word in terms of the other, quickly check the two valid quirky links:

1) Does one word provide a clear categorization of the other that's mimicked in the stem (e.g., *harmonious : music* and COHERENT : ARGUMENT)?
2) Are the two words clear variations on a single concept (e.g., *cottage : palace*)?

These quirky links are okay. But if the words don't fit either of those particular cases, ask yourself:

Do the two words have a "could be" relationship? A fake relationship? If so, the choice is a NO-DEF.

Accept no substitutes! Demand definitional links!

- -

At the beginning of the chapter, we saw the 4th step in our three-step process: Refine and Repeat.

However, it's better if you get the link right the first time—and with a little effort, you can.

✎ 4. Write good definitional links up front.

Remember "Push past neutral" in Antonyms? This is the same concept. Don't be lazy.

Push past these vague, weak links: 1 is part of 2
                                          1 uses 2 to work

How? In what way? **Focus on exact purpose, role, function, and position.** Then write your link.

However, despite your best intentions, you will still have to refine your first link from time to time.

Here is the best practice: **only refine after you check all the choices first** and eliminating non-matches, including NO-DEFs. Compare your refined link only to the surviving choices.

Some students (especially high-performers on Analogies) get nervous when they spot a divergence between their first link and the first answer choice or two. These students go back and try to refine their link too early. Instead, you should persevere with your first link until you've compared it to A through E. You'll probably be able to knock out a few wrong answers, which you should not bring back in the next round.

- -

Finally, if all else fails, we still have one more trick up our sleeve. It's a doozy.

When we work backwards from the answer choices, we can do more than just eliminate NO-DEFs.

✎ 5. Write links for the remaining answer choices and compare those links to the stem.

Make a guess as to whether the stem embodies the same relationship. If you think not, then the answer is probably wrong.

This approach should be your last resort. It consumes a lot of effort and time for limited reward.

However, it may help you get rid of 1–2 more wrong answers. That's all you need to improve your odds substantially.

Analogies Recap

⌐ **Three-Step Process**	1. Read only the stem.
	2. Write a simple linking sentence.
	3. Compare to each answer choice.
	4. Refine the link if necessary, and compare again.

⬚ Principles for Writing Links

- Good links could be in the dictionary.

- Part of speech can help. Use Noun subtypes (Person, Place, Thing, Quality, Action).

- Link types are DUCT Tape: Degree, Use, Characteristic, Type.

- Be aware of quirky links: push more meaning into the link, or define both words as versions of a 3rd thing.

- Learn Specialist 🔲 vocabulary.

To deal with hard vocab…

- Use the same tools as before for Double Agents 🔲, Rare Birds 🔲, Popular Pigeons 🔲, Root Sharks 🔲 & Minnows 🔲.

⚒ New Methods

⚒ Compare the link carefully to the answer choices.

⚒ Ignore vertical similarities among individual words. First construct horizontal relationships (the colons), then compare those relationships.

⚒ Eliminate NO-DEF 🔲–🔲 choices.

⚒ Write good definitional links up front. Only refine after checking all choices.

⚒ As a last resort, write links from answer choices and compare to the stem.

☠ New Traps

☠ Reversal: Wrong answer is right except for a subtle reversal.

☠ Spin/Strength: These factors are off.

☠ Smoke & Mirrors: Choices are superficially similar.

☠ Theme: Wrong answer is thematically related to the stem.

☠ Fake Relationship: Pair of words in wrong answer are related but not by definition.

Problem Set

Do these problems on a separate piece of paper. Remember to follow the three-step process!

1) NUCLEUS : ATOM ::

    (A) star : galaxy

    (B) kernel : corn

    (C) target : bullseye

    (D) yolk : egg

    (E) treasury : economy

2) CULPABLE : FAULT ::

    (A) disowned : treachery

    (B) meritorious : credit

    (C) intractable : conciliation

    (D) rebellious : sedition

    (E) pleasant : attraction

3) WAGGISH : WIT ::

    (A) loutish : impoliteness

    (B) autocratic : rue

    (C) miserly : resplendence

    (D) regal : honor

    (E) credulous : heresy

4) EMBEZZLER : TAKE ::

    (A) retiree : resign

    (B) apologist : vow

    (C) thief : steal

    (D) forger : duplicate

    (E) liberator : free

5) JOINTS : RHEUMATOLOGY ::

    (A) blood : dermatology

    (B) children : oncology

    (C) eyes : ophthalmology

    (D) cells : herpetology

    (E) health : cardiology

6) FISSURE : FAULT ::

    (A) felony : misdemeanor

    (B) dune : brook

    (C) cleft : palate

    (D) gap : blame

    (E) drizzle : monsoon

7) MILLINER : HATS ::

    (A) cowhand : cattle

    (B) cooper : barrels

    (C) fletcher : quiver

    (D) webster : loom

    (E) blacksmith : iron

8) ICEBERG : GLACIER ::

    (A) car : automobile

    (B) title : book

    (C) crumb : food

    (D) recital : symphony

    (E) drop : water

9) FRACTIOUS : CONTROL

   (A) impish : violate

   (B) bankrupt : spend

   (C) muddled : stir

   (D) burnished : shine

   (E) opaque : understand

10) INOCULATE : DISEASE ::

   (A) forge : escutcheon

   (B) weatherproof : rain

   (C) vaccinate : syringe

   (D) insulate : warmth

   (E) osculate : kiss

11) PLANTS : BOTANICAL ::

   (A) insects : entomological

   (B) grammar : etymological

   (C) women : anthropological

   (D) students : sociological

   (E) functions : biological

12) KING : REGICIDE ::

   (A) human : suicide

   (B) politician : patricide

   (C) exterminator : pesticide

   (D) mother : matricide

   (E) prisoner : homicide

13) GALOSH : FOOT ::

   (A) slicker : torso

   (B) waders : fish

   (C) suspenders : waist

   (D) parasol : lady

   (E) parka : leg

14) ERROR : SLIP ::

   (A) domicile : pieds-à-terre

   (B) fault : excuse

   (C) blunder : fall

   (D) melon : grape

   (E) idiot : ignoramus

15) VALEDICTION : SPEECH ::

   (A) wave : ocean

   (B) gustation : food

   (C) graduation : school

   (D) puissance : strength

   (E) ballad : song

16) REDUX : NASCENT ::

   (A) retrograde : direct

   (B) recondite : artistic

   (C) rebellious : faithful

   (D) recalcitrant : implacable

   (E) recidivist : criminal

17) FOOTLESS: SUBSTANCE ::

   (A) translucent : ghost

   (B) opalescent : cabochon

   (C) expurgated : improprieties

   (D) paradigmatic : model

   (E) shod : shoes

18) TALK : LOGORRHEIC ::

   (A) vegetate : verdurous

   (B) inundate : flooded

   (C) dispute : argumentative

   (D) speak : emblematic

   (E) crowd : agoraphobia

19) DEMUR : CHARY

   (A) drudge : heavy

   (B) mortify : embarrassed

   (C) articulate : expressed

   (D) prevaricate : misleading

   (E) variegate : cobbled

20) REVERENT : SANCTIMONIOUS

   (A) rational : pragmatic

   (B) thrifty : stingy

   (C) biased : dogmatic

   (D) refined: simplistic

   (E) creative : fantastical

1) D	2) B	3) A
4) D	5) C	6) E
7) B	8) C	9) E
10) B	11) A	12) D
13) A	14) A	15) E
16) E	17) C	18) C
19) D	20) B	

Sample links and various traps will be notated below.

1)   NUCLEUS : ATOM ::   1 = at the center of 2   (Characteristic)
     (A) star : galaxy   Theme
     (B) kernel : corn
     (C) target : bullseye   Reversal
     (D) yolk : egg   **Correct**
     (E) treasury : economy

2)   CULPABLE : FAULT ::   1 = deserving of 2   (Characteristic)
     (A) disowned : treachery   Fake Relationship, Theme
     (B) meritorious : credit   **Correct**
     (C) intractable : conciliation
     (D) rebellious : sedition
     (E) pleasant : attraction

3)   WAGGISH : WIT ::   1 = showing 2   (Characteristic)
     (A) loutish : impoliteness   **Correct**
     (B) autocratic : rue   NO-DEF
     (C) miserly : resplendence
     (D) regal : honor   NO-DEF
     (E) credulous : heresy   NO-DEF

4)   EMBEZZLER : TAKE ::   1 = someone who does 2 illegally   (Characteristic)
     (A) retiree : resign   NO-DEF, Fake Relationship
     (B) apologist : vow   NO-DEF
     (C) thief : steal   Theme, Spin. 1 = someone who does 2 (which already is illegal)
     (D) forger : duplicate   **Correct**
     (E) liberator : free   Spin. 1 = someone who does 2

5)   JOINTS : RHEUMATOLOGY ::   2 = study/treatment of 1   (Characteristic)
     (A) blood : dermatology
     (B) children : oncology   Fake Relationship (common phrase)
     (C) eyes : ophthalmology   **Correct**
     (D) cells : herpetology
     (E) health : cardiology   Fake Relationship (common phrase)

6) FISSURE : FAULT ::   1 = small version (of a gap), but 2 = large version (of a gap)   (Type, quirky)
    (A) felony : misdemeanor   Double Agent
    (B) dune : brook
    (C) cleft : palate   Theme, Fake Relationship
    (D) gap : blame   Theme, Double Agent (fault)
    (E) drizzle : monsoon   **Correct**

7) MILLINER : HATS ::   1 = creates 2   (Use/Purpose)
    (A) cowhand : cattle   Reversal (1 = works with 2)
    (B) cooper : barrels   **Correct**
    (C) fletcher : quiver
    (D) webster : loom   Reversal (1 = works with 2)
    (E) blacksmith : iron   Reversal (1 = works with 2)

8) ICEBERG : GLACIER ::   1 = small piece broken from 2   (Characteristic)
    (A) car : automobile
    (B) title : book   Reversal (1 = part of 2)
    (C) crumb : food   **Correct**
    (D) recital : symphony   Reversal (1 seems like "small" version of 2)
    (E) drop : water   Theme

9) FRACTIOUS : CONTROL   1= difficult to 2   (Characteristic)
    (A) impish : violate   Theme
    (B) bankrupt : spend   Theme, Spin (1 = result of doing too much 2)
    (C) muddled : stir   Spin (1 = result of 2)
    (D) burnished : shine
    (E) opaque : understand   **Correct**

10) INOCULATE : DISEASE ::   1 = protect something against harmful things such as 2   (Purpose)
    (A) forge : escutcheon
    (B) weatherproof : rain   **Correct**
    (C) vaccinate : syringe   Theme
    (D) insulate : warmth   Reversal (1 = keep good things in such as 2)
    (E) osculate : kiss

11) PLANTS : BOTANICAL ::   2 = descriptive of 1   (Characteristic)
    (A) insects : entomological   **Correct**
    (B) grammar : etymological   Fake Relationship
    (C) women : anthropological   NO-DEF
    (D) students : sociological   NO-DEF
    (E) functions : biological   Fake Relationship

12) KING : REGICIDE ::   2 = murder of 1   (Use/Purpose)
    (A) human : suicide   NO-DEF (2 = murder of 1, but not tight enough definition)
    (B) politician : patricide   NO-DEF
    (C) exterminator : pesticide   Reversal (1 uses 2 to kill)
    (D) mother : matricide   **Correct**
    (E) prisoner : homicide   Reversal, Fake Relationship (2 could result in 1 for someone)

13) GALOSH : FOOT ::   1 protects 2 against weather (rain)   (Use/Purpose)
   (A) slicker : torso   **Correct**
   (B) waders : fish   Theme
   (C) suspenders : waist
   (D) parasol : lady   Reversal (parasol is an umbrella, but for sun)
   (E) parka : leg

14) ERROR : SLIP ::   2 = small version of 1   (Type)
   (A) domicile : pieds-à-terre   **Correct**
   (B) fault : excuse   Theme
   (C) blunder : fall   Theme
   (D) melon : grape   Reversal (2 = large version of 3rd thing, fruit; 1 = small version)
   (E) idiot : ignoramus   Strength (same)

15) VALEDICTION : SPEECH ::   1 = type of 2   (Type)
   (A) wave : ocean   Reversal (1 = part of 2)
   (B) gustation : food
   (C) graduation : school   Theme
   (D) puissance : strength
   (E) ballad : song   **Correct**

16) REDUX : NASCENT ::   1 = being 2 again   (Degree)
   (A) retrograde : direct
   (B) recondite : artistic   Theme
   (C) rebellious : faithful
   (D) recalcitrant : implacable
   (E) recidivist : criminal   **Correct**
Also Smoke & Mirrors

17) FOOTLESS: SUBSTANCE ::   1 = lacking 2   (Characteristic)
   (A) translucent : ghost   Theme
   (B) opalescent : cabochon
   (C) expurgated : improprieties   **Correct**
   (D) paradigmatic : model   Reversal (1 = characterized by 2)
   (E) shod : shoes   Theme, Reversal

18) TALK : LOGORRHEIC ::   2 = tending to 1 a lot   (Characteristic)
   (A) vegetate : verdurous   Rare Bird (vegetate as verb + to be growing as a plant)
   (B) inundate : flooded   Reversal (2 = having been 1'd)
   (C) dispute : argumentative   **Correct**
   (D) speak : emblematic   NO-DEF
   (E) crowd : agoraphobia

19) DEMUR : CHARY   To 1 = to be 2   (Characteristic)
   (A) drudge : heavy   NO-DEF
   (B) mortify : embarrassed   Reversal (To 1 = cause someone else to be 2)
   (C) articulate : expressed   Reversal (To 1 = cause something to be 2)
   (D) prevaricate : misleading   **Correct**
   (E) variegate : cobbled   NO-DEF

20)   REVERENT : SANCTIMONIOUS   2 = excessively, negatively 1   (Degree)
       (A) rational : pragmatic   Spin/Strength
       (B) thrifty : stingy   **Correct**
       (C) biased : dogmatic   Spin/Strength
       (D) refined: simplistic
       (E) creative : fantastical

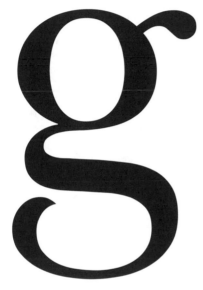

Chapter 5
of
ASA QUESTION TYPES

SENTENCE
COMPLETION

In This Chapter...

SENTENCE COMPLETION

Of the three ASA types, Sentence Completions probably seem the easiest to you. In fact, if you crunch the numbers published in the *Practicing to Take the GRE General Test, 10th Edition*, you'll find that the published Sentence Completions have a significantly lower average difficulty than any of the other Verbal types. (The other three Verbal types, including Reading Comprehension, have statistically indistinguishable difficulties.)

Why are Sentence Completions easier? Take a moment and try to define the word *cathartic*. Tough, right? Now, try to use the word in a sentence. This task is easier for most of us, because we understand the word in context. And if you read someone else's sentence including the word *cathartic,* you'd understand it right away. "I found the exam grueling but cathartic—in the end, it made me realize how much I love the English language!" (By the way, *cathartic* means "releasing tension, purging negative emotions through an intense experience.")

In Antonyms, it was you against the word. In Analogies, you had two words, so you could work out a relationship. In Sentence Completion, you have an entire sentence to work with! That's why Sentence Completion is a little easier.

Here's what a Sentence Completion problem looks like.

Xxxxx xx xxx _____ xxxx x xxx xxxxxxx _____ xxx xxx xxx xxx,
xx xxxxx xxxx xx x xx xxxxxxxxx xxx xx.

(A) ~~~. . ~~~
(B) ~~~. . ~~~
(C) ~~~. . ~~~
(D) ~~~. . ~~~
(E) ~~~. . ~~~

Your task is to find the choice that **best fits the meaning** of the sentence as a whole.

The sentence could have one or two blanks. There is almost always just one word per blank.

As you might expect by this point, all the words fitting into a blank have the same part of speech.

And as you know by now, the best approach will be to **anticipate an answer** before looking at the choices. Many people don't do this. Rather, they just plug the choices in one by one, rereading the sentence and stopping when it "sounds good."

Here's how you can tell: looking at the Sentence Completions published in the Official Guide, we know that SC problems with right answer A are, on average, significantly easier than SC problems with right answer E. 27% of test takers got "A-problems" wrong, whereas 46% of test takers got "E-problems" wrong—almost twice as many!

Do you think that the GRE deliberately wrote problems with correct answer E to be that much harder than problems with correct answer A? That's very unlikely. What's probably happening is that people are lazy. If you don't predict the answer and just plug the choices instead—and the correct answer is A—then you get lucky. The sentence probably makes sense, and you pick A. On the other hand, if the right answer is E, then your lack of good process punishes you. You waste a lot of time plugging and re-reading, you get confused, and you go off the rails.

So follow the three-step process below to give yourself the best chance of getting any question right!

⌐ Three-Step Process for Sentence Correction

Let's look at a straightforward example.

> If the student had been less _____, he would not have been expelled from his grade school.
>
> (A) indefatigable
> (B) perseverant
> (C) refractory
> (D) playful
> (E) indigent

1. Read only the sentence.

At this point, you should know that the answer choices will distract you if you read them before you've made sense of the question.

2. Find the clue and the pivot, and write down your own filler.

The clue and the pivot are the two most important parts of the sentence.

The clue is what forces the contents of the blank to be perfectly predictable. In other words, the clue solves the mystery of the blank. Look for dramatic action or emotion.

In this case, the clue is *expelled*.

The pivot is what determines the relationship between the blank and the pivot. Will the blank agree with the clue? Or will the blank actually disagree with the clue? It depends on the pivot.

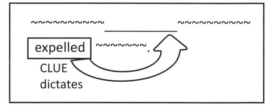

The sentence reads *less _____ ...not expelled.* So the pivot is *less...not*.

Think about what this means. If the student were *less such-and-such*, then he would *not* have been expelled.

So such-and-such got him expelled. In other words, the blank agrees with *expelled. Less* and *not* cancel each other out as negatives.

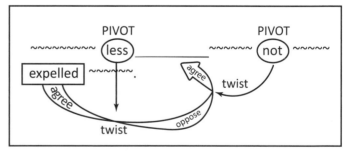

Finally, **the filler is what you predict the answer to be.** At this point, how would you describe this student using the blank? Write down this adjective or phrase, as well as your A through E.

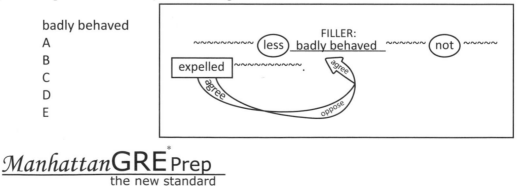

badly behaved
A
B
C
D
E

3. Compare to each answer choice.

Here are the choices again. One at a time, insert the word into the blank, match to your filler, and mark down Good, Bad, Sort Of, or Unknown.

        (A) indefatigable = tireless
        (B) perseverant = determined, unstoppable
        (C) refractory = ??
        (D) playful
        (E) indigent = poor

So now your paper might look like this.

          badly behaved
          ~~A~~
          ~~B~~
          C ?
          D ~
          E ~

The correct answer is in fact C, since *refractory* means "rebellious." Even if you didn't know what *refractory* means, you would have a good shot at getting this problem right through process of elimination. Also notice that you can imagine an interesting story around some of the wrong answer choices. If the student had been less *playful*, he wouldn't have been expelled? What went wrong in some game? Or if the student had been less *indigent*, he wouldn't have been expelled? How horrible—what an indictment of the administration of the school.

We should put our natural desire for good stories out of our head when we do Sentence Completions. What we want for our filler is **complete predictability and redundancy**. There should be no surprises in the blank—after all, this is a standardized test, and there is only one right answer. **Avoid interesting stories!**

Sentence Completions versus Analogies and Antonyms

    Bad News: **There is still tough vocabulary, with all the attendant tricks.**

Your mastery of the Word Beasts is still the biggest single factor that will determine your success on the problem. The various vocabulary traps are still around.

However, as we've already noted…

    Good News: **You get a lot of context for the vocabulary.**

Sentence Completion is the most forgiving of the three ASA types if you don't know the word in question. Moreover, the traps are less varied than on the other two types.

The context does have its drawbacks.

    Bad News: **The sentences require time to read.**

Some of these sentences are pretty long. You might guess that longer sentences are harder.

That proves not to be true. In fact, what seems to be the case is that the extra reading burden is offset by the fact that long sentences give you more clues to the right answer.

What does all this mean?

> **A. You still need to work on your vocabulary.**
>
> **B. Good process, as before, solves most issues.**

How To Write Good Fillers

As you try to write good fillers, keep in mind the following simple equation:

⏛ Filler = Clue + Pivot

The filler is nothing more interesting than a simple sum, so to speak, of the clue and the pivot.

Let's walk through an example.

> In the past decade, the coffee chain has dramatically expanded all across the country, leading one commentator to describe the franchise as _____.

First, find the clue. There could be more than one. The clue is often the most descriptive part of the sentence (e.g., *expelled*). You will often also see judgment calls as clues.

In the sentence above, *dramatically expanded* is the clue.

Next, find the pivot. Again, the pivot determines the relationship between the clue and the filler. The two most common possibilities are these:

1) The filler **agrees with** the clue. This is the default.
2) The filler **opposes** the clue. The pivot will express negation or opposition.

The pivot could also indicate a causal relation or some other type, but even then, you can often get away with simply determining whether the filler and the clue agree or disagree.

In the sentence above, nothing indicates opposition between the filler and the clue. If anything, words such as *leading* and *describe* point you toward simple agreement.

So we need a blank that expresses agreement with *dramatically expanded*.

Finally, construct the filler out of the clue and the pivot. Recycle words if possible. This instinct will keep you from straying too far from the given meaning of the sentence. Feel free to use a phrase.

Your filler might literally be this: having dramatically expanded

Be ready to **change the part of speech**, if necessary.

Or you might have gone just a little further: everywhere

Notice how uninteresting this filler makes the sentence. Don't over-think. In real life, you could easily imagine the filler taking you substantially further than *having dramatically expanded*. For instance, the commentator may add a negative spin (*overreached*), but the GRE will make the filler much more boring in meaning. **Assume as little as possible.**

The word "filler" should make you think of something uninteresting. That's the right way to go.

A likely answer would be something like *ubiquitous*, a GRE favorite.

Pivot Words

Fill in your own word in this sentence:

> Despite his reputation for _____, the politician decided that in a time of crisis it was important to speak honestly and forthrightly.

Did you say something like "not being direct"? The pivot word *despite* indicates an *opposite direction*. *Honestly and forthrightly* was the judgment call about the politician. Since the pivot was negative, we pivoted *away* from *honestly and forthrightly*.

> For all her studying, her performance on the test was _____.

This one relies on an idiom. Did you say something like "mediocre" or "bad"? The expression *for all X, Y* is in play here. *For all* here means "despite." Thus, despite her studying, her performance was *not good*.

> Although he has a reputation for volubility, others at the party didn't find him to be especially _____.

Did you say something like "talkative"? Or did you go for "not talkative"? Notice we have a judgment call (*volubility*, which means "talkativeness") and a pivot word, *although*. But we also have another pivot—the *not* in *didn't*. Pivoting twice (much like turning 180 degrees, twice) is like not pivoting at all. In our blank, we just want another word for *talkative*.

Here are some common pivot words, phrases, and structures.

SAME DIRECTION	**OPPOSITE DIRECTION**	**CAUSAL RELATIONSHIP**
And	But	Because
Also	Despite	Therefore
Furthermore	Although	Thus
Moreover	In spite of	Hence
Besides	Rather than	So
In addition	Nevertheless	Consequently
Not only … but also	Still	As a result
Just as … as	Though	
So … as to be	Yet	
In fact	On the other hand	
: (colon)	On the contrary	
; (semicolon)	Whether X or Y	
X, Y, and Z (items in a list)		

Two Blanks Can Be Better Than One

Two-blank sentences are more common than one-blank sentences. Nearly two thirds of the questions in the Official Guide have two blanks. Again, these may seem harder because they are often longer, but there are more clues. Also, having two clues means that there are generally two paths: a harder path and an easier path.

Which path would you rather take?

⚒ Start with the easier blank.

Don't just try to fill in the first blank automatically. Look at both blanks and figure out which one has an easier clue. Then create a filler and use that filler as an extra clue for the harder blank.

Let's go through an example.

> Even seasoned opera singers, who otherwise affect an
> unflappable air, can be _____ performing in Rome, where
> audiences traditionally view _____ performers as a birthright,
> passed down from heckler to heckler over generations.

Blank #2 is easier. Why? Compare the clues and pivots:

	Clues	**Pivots**	
Blank #1:	*seasoned* *unflappable*	*even...otherwise...*	The pivots express opposition. What is the opposite of *unflappable*?
Blank #2:	*heckler*	none	No pivot = agreement

Our filler for #2 should probably be *heckling*. Remember to reuse the given language in the filler when you can.

Now we can use that filler as another clue. There is no pivot between the two blanks, meaning that the two fillers agree in some way. The relationship seems to be causal: the opera performers are going to react to that heckling. A likely filler would be *upset by* or *afraid of.*

Our paper might now look like this: afraid of...heckling

Now compare to the answer choices and mark your paper.

> (A) intrepid about. .jeering
> (B) displeased by. .extolling
> (C) enthusiastic about. .lionizing
> (D) daunted by. .badgering
> (E) grateful for. .acknowledging

Alternatively, you could have narrowed down the list by doing two rounds of comparison, using the filler you first got (*heckling*) to eliminate (B), (C), and (E). The filler for the first blank gets us the rest of the way: the correct answer is (D).

Finally, **watch out for and avoid 1-sided matches.** You might have liked *jeering* in (A) a bit better than *badgering* in (D), but both sides must match well enough.

Tricky Aspects of the Sentence

Take a look at this example.

> Although Paula claimed not to be _____ that she was not
> selected for the scholarship, we nevertheless worried that
> our typically sanguine friend was not entirely _____ by the
> decision.

This sentence is just chock-full of switchbacks. Count the oppositional pivots: *Although…not…nevertheless… typically…not entirely…*

It's easy to lose your way in a thicket of **Double-Negative Pivots**, especially under exam pressure. How many wrongs make a right?

When you face a situation such as this…

⚒ Break it down.

Chop up the sentence and process it in small chunks. You can't rewrite the sentence, but focus on bits at a time. Start with the earliest or the most concrete part of the story. Then add one chunk at a time. Change complicated pivots to simple words, such as *but* and *so*.

As you go, emotionally punctuate each part of the story. Exaggerate the switchbacks in your mental voice, as if you were telling a story you really cared about. Reword as you go, if you must. Finally, as you think about the whole, discard unnecessary elements, so you don't have to hold everything in your head at once.

For the sentence above, the breakdown might go like this.

> Our friend Paula is *typically* sanguine = optimistic ☺
>
> She was not selected for a scholarship ☹
>
> She claimed NOT to be _____
>
> BUT
>
> We still worried ☹
>
> that she was NOT entirely _____ by the decision.

The fillers should be pretty easy to generate now: *upset/saddened* ☹ for the first blank, and *unaffected* for the second.

It looks like a lot of work, but your brain can generate this train of thought in seconds. Give it a try.

Other tricky aspects of the sentence yield to the same basic medicine: **Break it Down**. Give each sentence a try. Sample fillers are on the next page.

Unfamiliar Style or Content

"That such a _____ of precedent would be countenanced was itself unprecedented in the court, a bastion of traditionalism."

> The sentence starts with a *That* clause, a hallmark of a very academic, written style. Moreover, the content is about a legal matter. These two factors combine with difficult vocabulary (*precedent, countenanced, bastion*) to make the sentence forbidding.

Red Herring Clues

"By rigorously observing social behavior, anthropologists _____ strict, though implicit, codes of conduct."

> A few "clues" might not really be clues. The word *strict* turns out to be less important to the answer than *implicit*. Decoy answers might be *undermine* or *challenge* (somehow dealing with the *strict* element, but introducing too much new information in the filler).

Blanks in Tough Spots

"If these managers _____ the advantages of the new deep-sea recovery methodology to be _____ then it will rapidly be judged less useful than current alternatives by the broader business community."

> Some blanks are positioned in such a way that it's hard to hold the sentence in your head. The gaps occur early or in strategic places. For instance, in the sentence above, the verb of the first clause is missing. In contrast, some easier questions let you formulate the thought relatively easily without the words in the blank or blanks.

Synonym Disguises

> The sentence employs synonyms (even outside of direct clues and the blanks) to disguise the meaning of the whole.

> Notice in the previous example that the words *advantages* and *useful* are connected by a Synonym Disguise.

Again, the medicine is the same, no matter what. You simply have to make sense of the sentence, and the best way to do that is to **break it down into pieces and make sense of the parts**. Reword or simplify if you have to.

For the sentences above, possible fillers include the following:

> "That such a <u>rejection</u> of precedent…"
> "… anthropologists <u>reveal, make explicit</u> strict, though implicit…"
> "If these managers <u>find</u> the advantages… to be <u>lacking</u>, then…"

Traps to Avoid During Elimination

As you go through the three-step process and select an answer, be on the lookout for the following traps, which are variations of what you've seen before in your work with Antonyms and Analogies.

Give the following problem a try.

The event horizon, or boundary, of a black hole represents both _____ and intangibility; space travelers would pass through this literal "point of no return" so _____ that the precise moment at which their fate was sealed would almost certainly not be registered.

      (A) mystery. .dangerously
      (B) inconsequentiality. .imminently
      (C) hazard. .heroically
      (D) irrevocability. .indiscernibly
      (E) infallibility. .imperceptibly

Which is the easier blank?

Most would agree that the second blank is easier. The clue is *the moment… would not be registered*, and the lack of a pivot tells us that the filler agrees with the clue. So we might fill in something like *without registering* (again, recycling language from the sentence itself).

Turning to the first blank, we can see that the *without registering* filler lines up with *intangibility*, while the first blank lines up with "point of no return." So we might fill in *no return* for the first blank.

Now we match to the answer choices. Both (D) and (E) match the second filler (*without registering*), but only *irrevocability* fits *no return*. The correct answer is (D).

Notice the trap language in (A), (B), and (C): *mystery, dangerously, imminently, heroically*. It's possible that you might construct a narrative around the question that would make some of these trap answers appealing. We've seen this trap before in Antonyms.

☠ *Theme Trap*

    = Wrong answer choice shares a theme or field with the sentence.

Broader "Smoke & Mirrors" is rarer on Sentence Completion, but the Theme trap variation is prevalent. The word is in a common phrase or association with part of the sentence. As a result, the choice sounds okay on its own and somehow "together" with the sentence, even though it doesn't really fit the blanks.

The way to avoid this trap is simple. **Stick to the basic process.** If you had anticipated the answers, you would have been able to eliminate (A), (B), and (C) without ever worrying about the thematic connections.

Now try this problem.

Marie was nettled by her sister's constant jocularity and preferred a _____ approach to life.

      (A) pessimistic
      (B) grim
      (C) waggish
      (D) staid
      (E) sycophantic

It was probably pretty easy for you to identify the clues (*nettled, jocularity, preferred*) and to see that Marie is against *jocularity* or joking behavior. A filler might be *serious.*

Now, imagine that you go through the answer choices. *Pessimistic* and *grim* both "sort of" match, but they both seem to go too far. Just because Marie doesn't like her sister's constant joking, must she be *pessimistic* or *grim* in her outlook on life? Not necessarily. Perhaps you don't remember what *waggish* or *staid* mean, and you don't totally remember *sycophantic* either, but you're sure it doesn't mean *serious.*

So your paper might look like this:

> serious
> A ~
> B ~
> C ?
> D ?
> E ✗

We can now identify another trap. You don't like *pessimistic* or *grim,* but you don't know the other words, so you find yourself reluctant to choose (C) or (D). Unfortunately, you're falling into a trap...

☠ *Easy But Not Close Enough Trap*

> = Wrong answer choice is "in the ballpark" but something is off in the meaning.
> However, the word is familiar, so it's attractive.

You might be afraid to pick a word you don't know. **Overcome this fear.** As it turns out, the correct answer is (D) *staid,* which does mean "serious, sedate by temperament or habits."

You will also see **Reversal traps** (you miss a pivot or mix up a negative). This is a matter of attention to detail in the moment.

Finally, don't forget all our fun **vocab traps**! All our Word Beasts are still flying around in Sentence Completion. Again, though, the context of the sentence will help you solve lots of problems that arise purely from vocabulary.

Two Blanks and No Clue

It's very rare but possible that, in a two-blank sentence, the two blanks function as clues for each other, but there's no good outside clue. As a result, the sentence can be read in a few different ways.

> If the boss _____ John's expense report, then John is likely to be _____.

In this case, you have two options.

Option A: Determine the Relationship

This is similar to Analogies, but much, much simpler. The two blanks usually *agree* or *oppose,* perhaps causally. Then eliminate choices.

For instance, in the case above, the two blanks agree causally. The boss's reaction dictates what happens to John. A couple of possible pairs are *loves. .promoted* or *hates. .fired.*

This option sounds great in theory, but it can actually be difficult to pull off. If you get stuck, try the next option.

Option B: Plug #1 and Predict #2

Look at the choices one at a time.

For each choice, take blank #1 as given in the choice. This eliminates a variable.

Now predict what blank #2 should be. Pretend that you temporarily have a one-blank problem, and you need just one filler. Come up with your filler, and then compare it to the given #2.

This process may seem to take more time on paper, but in practice it can be quite fast. Each step is easy and quick to process.

Sentence Completion Recap

⊿ **Three-Step Process**	1. Read only the sentence. 2. Find the clue and pivot, and write down your own filler. 3. Compare to each answer choice.

Principle for Writing Fillers

- Filler = Clue + Pivot. Reuse material from the sentence.

Principle for Two Blanks

- Start with the easier blank. Avoid 1-sided matches.

✕ **Methods**	☠ **Traps (New and Old)**
✕ Break down tricky sentences.	☠ Double Negative Pivots ☠ Unfamiliar Style/Content ☠ Red Herring Clues ☠ Blanks in Tough Spots ☠ Synonym Disguises
✕ Stick to the basic process as you eliminate.	☠ Theme: Wrong answer is thematically related to the stem. ☠ Easy But Not Close Enough: familiar, attractive word that's clearly off in some way. ☠ Reversal (pivots)
✕ Two Blanks and No Clue	

        Option A: Determine the Relationship (as for Analogies).
        Option B: Plug #1 and Predict #2.

Problem Set

Do these problems on a separate piece of paper. Remember to follow the three-step process!

1)   Professor Honeycutt was known as a probing questioner of her students; she always wanted to get to the _____ of any intellectual matter.

   (A) emotions
   (B) academics
   (C) pith
   (D) periphery
   (E) examination

2)   Though she had made attempts towards adopting a more _____ lifestyle, she was not above indulging her proclivities towards _____ dishes.

   (A) frugal. .edible
   (B) truculent. .delectable
   (C) salubrious. .odious
   (D) wholesome. .iniquitous
   (E) salutary. .succulent

3)   While she was known to all her friends as quite the _____ her private behavior belied this _____ image.

   (A) sage. .stodge
   (B) raconteur. .genial
   (C) socialite. .belligerent
   (D) educator. .pedantic
   (E) curmudgeon. .whimsical

4)   In determining the defendant's sentencing, the jury will take into account whether he acted on _____ motives or instead took risks to deflect the kingpin's reprisal from the neighborhood in a truly altruistic way.

   (A) ulterior
   (B) criminal
   (C) recidivist
   (D) lucrative
   (E) selfish

5)   The doctor's presentation at the conference gave numerous suggestions for incurring the _____ of the treatment while obviating damage to auxiliary structures.

   (A) diagnosis
   (B) mien
   (C) prognosis
   (D) costs
   (E) benefits

6)   The university president argued that top universities should not _____ education as an academic _____ discouraging our brightest students from pursuing teaching careers does a disservice to the next generation of students.

   (A) proscribe. .recommendation
   (B) disdain. .discipline
   (C) circumvent. .field
   (D) deign. .subject
   (E) disavow. .topic

7)   The new film, though a chronicle of exploitation and iniquity, nevertheless is deeply concerned with notions of _____ eventually showcasing the elimination of all the protagonist's abusers, granting the audience the _____ they've been awaiting for two hours.

   (A) fairness. .inconclusiveness
   (B) inequity. .relief
   (C) justice. .catharsis
   (D) slavery. .freedom
   (E) equality. .credit

8)   The fact that bringing together criminals and their victims for a moderated conversation has been shown to vastly reduce rates of _____ can be explained by the fact that those who commit crimes can only do so by convincing themselves their actions have no _____.

   (A) violence. .resonance
   (B) birth. .inconsistencies
   (C) malfeasance. .consequences
   (D) reoffending. .source
   (E) recidivism. .ramifications

9)   The _____ of the word *assassin* is _____ in philological circles, as the word comes from a sect of brutal killers believed to have smoked the drug hashish before going on a mission.

   (A) introduction. .enigmatic
   (B) use. .forbidden
   (C) history. .known
   (D) derivation. .notorious
   (E) etymology. .unheralded

10)   Though she acknowledges that modern farming practices are more _____ than traditional agriculture, she nonetheless argues that this difference represents no real _____.

   (A) expensive. .improvement
   (B) productive. .secret
   (C) polluting. .advantage
   (D) efficient. .progress
   (E) profitable. .disincentive

1) C   2) E   3) B
4) A   5) E   6) B
7) C   8) E   9) D
10) D

1) Professor Honeycutt was known as a ⌐probing questioner¬ of her students; she always wanted to get to the
heart, core of any intellectual matter.   clue   pivot = agree

     (A) emotions
     (B) academics
     (C) pith **Correct.**
     (D) periphery
     (E) examination

opposing pivot

2) ⌐Though¬ she had made attempts towards adopting a more healthy lifestyle, she was ⌐not above¬ ⌐indulging¬
her proclivities towards nonhealthy dishes.   pivot   clue

     (A) frugal. .edible
     (B) truculent. .delectable
     (C) salubrious. .odious
     (D) wholesome. .iniquitous
     (E) salutary. .succulent **Correct.**

                                           agree

3) While she was known to all her friends as quite the noun, her private behavior belied this adjective image.
                                   no outside clue

     (A) sage. .stodge
     (B) raconteur. .genial Agree. **Correct.**
     (C) socialite. .belligerent
     (D) educator. .pedantic
     (E) curmudgeon. .whimsical

4) In determining the defendant's sentencing, the jury will take into account whether he acted on selfish, self-
interested motives ⌐or instead¬ took risks to deflect the kingpin's reprisal from the neighborhood in a truly
                      opposing pivot
⌐altruistic¬ way.
   clue

     (A) ulterior
     (B) criminal
     (C) recidivist
     (D) lucrative
     (E) selfish **Correct.**

5)   The doctor's presentation at the conference gave numerous [suggestions] for incurring the <u>benefits</u> of the
clue

treatment [while | obviating] damage to auxiliary structures.
balancing pivot   clue

(A) diagnosis
(B) mien
(C) prognosis
(D) costs
(E) benefits **Correct.**

6)   The university president argued that top universities should not <u>put down</u> education as an academic <u>career,</u>

<u>endeavor</u>; [discouraging] our brightest students from [pursuing teaching careers] does a disservice to the
no pivot   clue   clue

next generation of students.

(A) proscribe. .recommendation
(B) disdain. .discipline **Correct.**
(C) circumvent. .field
(D) deign. .subject
(E) disavow. .topic

7)   opposing pivot   clue
The new film, [though] a chronicle of [exploitation] and iniquity, nevertheless is deeply concerned with

notions of <u>non-exploitation</u>, [eventually] showcasing the [elimination of all the protagonist's abusers],
clue   clue

granting the audience the <u>release</u> they've been awaiting for two hours.

(A) fairness. .inconclusiveness
(B) inequity. .relief
(C) justice. .catharsis **Correct.**
(D) slavery. .freedom
(E) equality. .credit

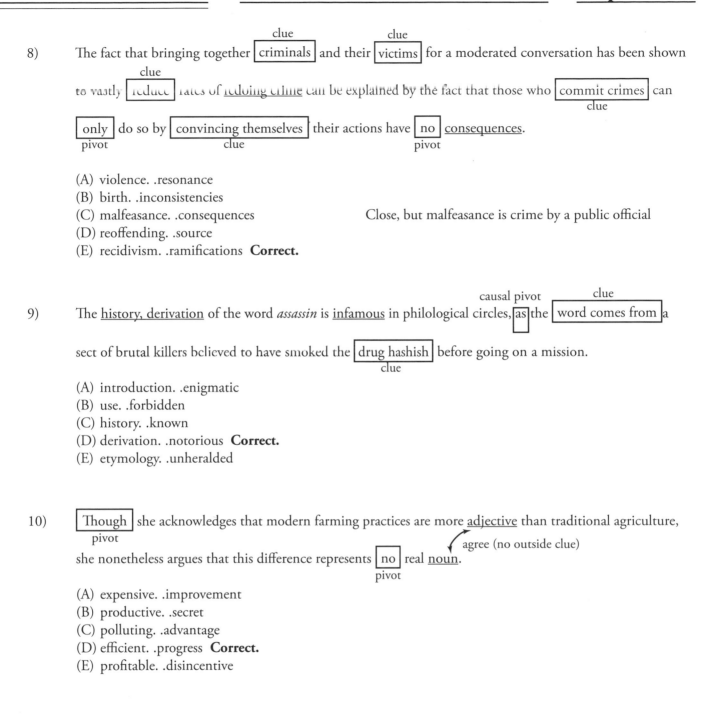

8) The fact that bringing together criminals and their victims for a moderated conversation has been shown

to vastly reduce rates of reducing crime can be explained by the fact that those who commit crimes can

only do so by convincing themselves their actions have no consequences.

(A) violence. .resonance
(B) birth. .inconsistencies
(C) malfeasance. .consequences   Close, but malfeasance is crime by a public official
(D) reoffending. .source
(E) recidivism. .ramifications **Correct.**

9) The history, derivation of the word *assassin* is infamous in philological circles, as the word comes from a

sect of brutal killers believed to have smoked the drug hashish before going on a mission.

(A) introduction. .enigmatic
(B) use. .forbidden
(C) history. .known
(D) derivation. .notorious **Correct.**
(E) etymology. .unheralded

10) Though she acknowledges that modern farming practices are more adjective than traditional agriculture,

agree (no outside clue)

she nonetheless argues that this difference represents no real noun.

(A) expensive. .improvement
(B) productive. .secret
(C) polluting. .advantage
(D) efficient. .progress **Correct.**
(E) profitable. .disincentive

Appendix

of

ASA QUESTION TYPES

In This Chapter ...

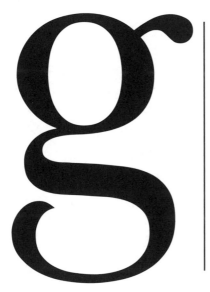

- Visual Dictionary
- Roots List
- Sneak Peak at the August 2011 GRE

Military

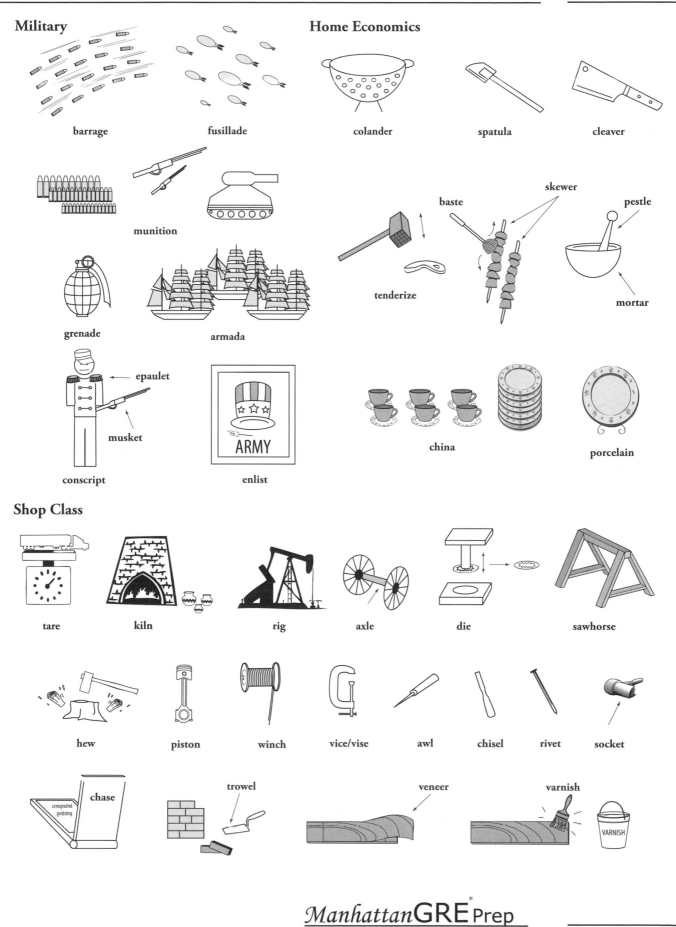

barrage

fusillade

munition

grenade

armada

conscript

epaulet

musket

enlist

Home Economics

colander

spatula

cleaver

baste

skewer

pestle

tenderize

mortar

china

porcelain

Shop Class

tare

kiln

rig

axle

die

sawhorse

hew

piston

winch

vice/vise

awl

chisel

rivet

socket

chase

trowel

veneer

varnish

APPENDIX VISUAL DICTIONARY

Professions

cartwright

vintner

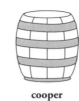
cooper

surveyor

fletcher

philatelist

numismatist

blacksmith

cobbler

cartographer

chandler

milliner

porter

webster

tanner

cowhand

Textiles & Clothes

ruffle

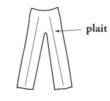
fringe

plait

sash

cravat

tassel

lace

filligree

sampler

embroider

stitch

crochet

skein

spool

flax

linen

loom

ManhattanGRE Prep
the new standard

Science & Medicine

Medicine & Chemistry

Anatomy

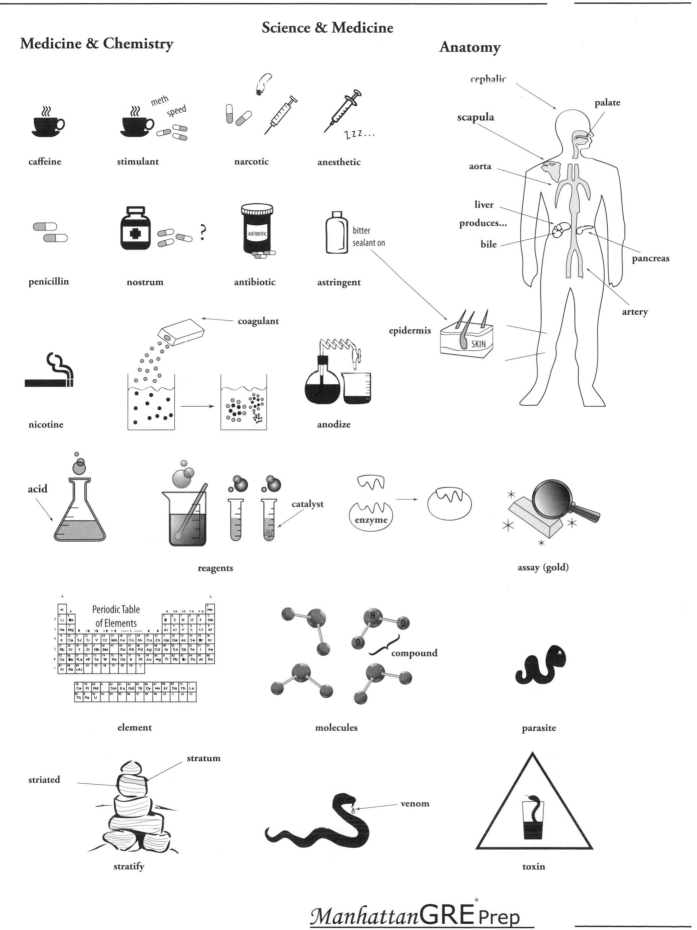

caffeine

stimulant

narcotic

anesthetic

penicillin

nostrum

antibiotic

astringent

nicotine

coagulant

anodize

acid

reagents

catalyst

enzyme

assay (gold)

element

molecules

compound

parasite

striated

stratum

stratify

venom

toxin

cephalic

palate

scapula

aorta

liver produces... bile

pancreas

artery

epidermis

SKIN

Science & Medicine

Processes

vaporize

acid + base → salt
neutralization

respiration

palpitate

resuscitation

blood vessel
hemorrhage

osmosis

fermentation WINE

distillate

Specialties

podiatry

SUN SCREEN R
dermatology

cardiology

pathology

oncology

neurology

Tools

lancet

scalpel

syringe

pediatrics

calipers

centrifuge

tourniquet

homeopathy

ELIXIR OF LIFE
alchemy

Pisces Taurus
astrology

ecology

Government

Government by...

...scientists, technicians

one person

...the people

technocracy

monarchy

democracy

...a few

oligarchy

...the rich

...the old

...an elite

plutocracy

gerontocracy

aristocracy

enfranchise

CORRUPTION
graft

interregnum

2012   2013 2014 2015

Law

writ

subpoena

statute

TRANSFER PROPERTY
deed

preamble

levy

magistrate

mace

gavel

Business & Accounting

ledger

securities

amortize

portfolio

accrue

CAN FORECLOSE
lien

Senate

"talk..."
filibuster

MAJORITY
SENATE
quorum

øte!
cloture

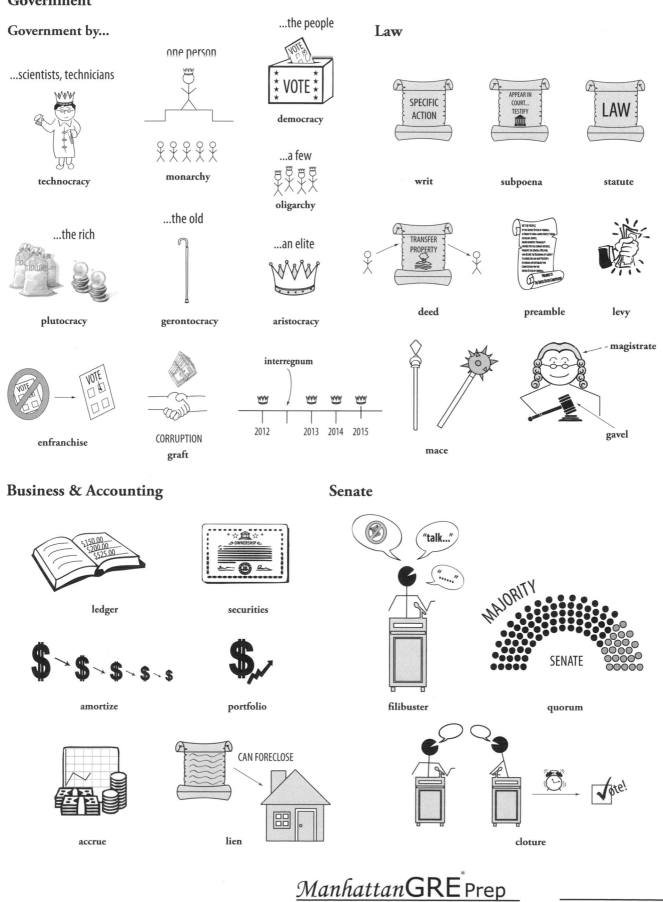

Architecture

truss

aqueduct

keystone

buttress

pylon

or

pylon

basilica

arabesque

levee

statuary

epitaph

guy

recess

fresco

parquetry

alcove

Architecture

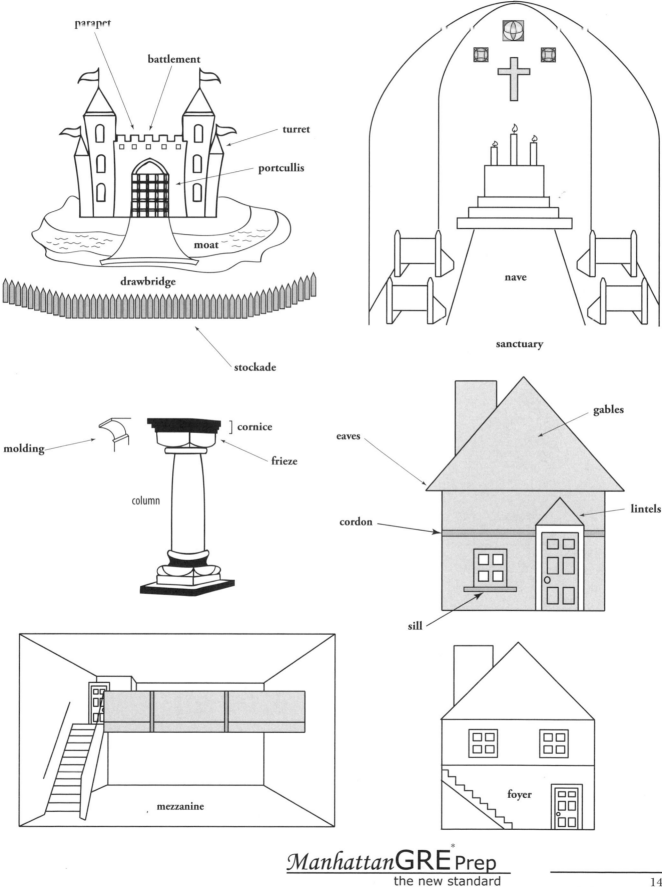

Media & The Arts

palette

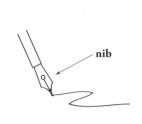

nib

homiletics

crescendo

troupe

pirouette

burlesque

soliloquy

"To be, or not to be…"

Hamlet

recital

IMPROVISE

extemporize

duet

light   parody   short   satire

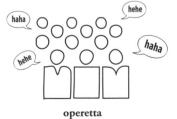

haha   hehe   hehe   haha

operetta

aria

opera

Media & The Arts

Types of Poems

symphony or opera

sonata

elegy

dirge

stanza

RIP

CAST

credits

sonnet

haha...???

doggerel

A
A
B
B
A

haha

limerick

Summaries

anthology

FIELD OF KNOWLEDGE

compendium

4-hour meeting

one page

précis

POEMS

lyric

NEWS
By A. GRE

byline

daguerreotype

Philosophy

knowledge

truth   belief

"If a tree falls in a forest..."

How do we know?

epistemology

SUBJECTIVE

"red" "smooth"
"sweet"
"soft"

OBJECTIVE

2.2"

2.5"

5 lbs.

phenomenology

"What is ?..."

"I think, therefore I am"

existence   reality

metaphysics

Dimensions & Units

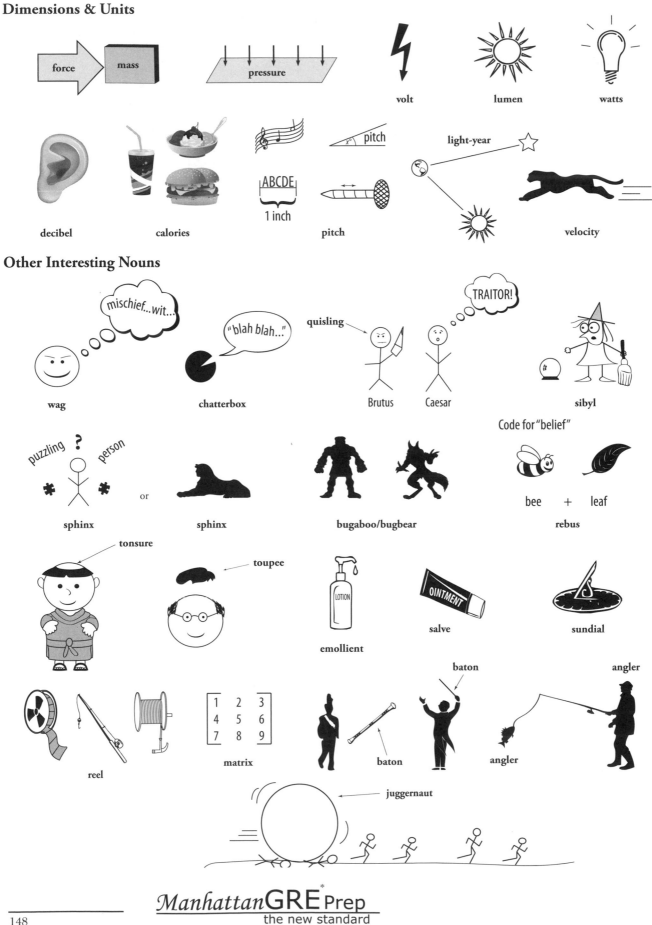

Roots List

Many words in English, especially those that come from Latin or Greek, have more than one part. Here is the basic pattern:

Word	=	Prefix	+	Root	+	Suffix
EXCISION	=	EX	+	CIS	+	ION

The root contains the original core meaning of the word, although this meaning may have changed over time. Here, the root *cis* means "cut."

The prefix alters that meaning in some way. Here, the prefix *ex-* means "out" or "away."

Together, the prefix and the root handle most of the meaning. *Ex* + *cis* = excise, or "cut away."

Finally, the suffix determines the part of speech. The suffix *–ion* means "the action of doing X," so *excision* means "the act of cutting away."

Be careful! Many words do NOT so neatly decompose into parts. The original meaning of the whole word may have only been related metaphorically to the meaning of its components. Moreover, over time, many words have changed tremendously in meaning.

Study roots, prefixes, and suffixes primarily to solidify your vocabulary. On the test, you can and should use your root knowledge to guess at the meaning of unknown words. Realize, however, that the GRE loves Root Sharks that can trick you. Be sure to learn the full dictionary meanings of vocabulary words.

Part I: Roots

This list includes a broad selection of roots and illustrative examples that often appear on the GRE. The examples have been chosen specifically to illustrate the root and thus to avoid meaning drift. Nearly all the roots are Latin or Greek. This list is not exhaustive; it is meant to provide a useful reference.

The definitions given for the harder words are brief. Remember to consult your dictionary for nuances.

Root	Meaning	Examples
ac	sharp *or*	**ac**id
acer	point *or*	**acr**id = sharp, bitter (of smell or taste)
acri	high	**acer**bity = bitterness
acro		**acri**mony = sharpness of words, behavior, or feeling
		acme = highest point, best level
		acrophobia = "high + fear" = fear of heights
		acumen = sharpness of intellect
ag	drive *or*	**ag**ent, **act**
act	lead *or*	dem**ag**ogue = "people + lead" = leader who appeals (falsely) to the people
	do	re**act** = do in response

Root	Meaning	Examples
alt	high	**alt**itude, **alt**imeter ex**alt**ed = "out + high" = raised high
ambul	walk	circum**ambul**ate = "around + walk" = walk around in a circle per**ambul**ate = "through + walk" = walk through, inspect
anim	spirit *or* breath	**anim**ate un**anim**ous = "one + spirit" = in complete agreement equ**anim**ity = "even + spirit" = calmness, balance under stress magn**anim**ity = "great + spirit" = nobility of spirit pusill**anim**ous = "tiny + spirit" = cowardly, without courage
arch	rule	an**arch**y = "not + ruler" = chaos, lack of government
aud	hear	**aud**ience, **aud**ible **aud**itory = related to hearing
bell belli	war	re**bell**ion **belli**cose = ready to fight, warlike **belli**gerent = "war + do" – hostile, provocative, or actually at war
cad cid	fall	de**cad**ent = "away + fall" = in a state of decline, often self-indulgent re**cid**ivism = "back + fall" = tendency to relapse to earlier behavior or crime
ced cess ceed	go *or* yield	pro**ceed**, suc**ceed**, ex**ceed**, re**ced**e **ced**e = yield ante**ced**ent = "before + go" = earlier event or cause pre**ced**ent = "before + go" = earlier example **cess**ation = end of an action
chron	time	**chron**ological, **chron**ic ana**chron**ism = "not + time" = something out of place in time dia**chron**ic = "through + time" = relating to change over time
cis cide	cut *or* kill	in**cis**ive = "into + cut" = cutting to the heart of a matter, direct ex**cis**ion = "out + cut" = act of cutting out, removing regi**cid**e = "king + kill" = murder of a king
clud clus claus	close	in**clud**e, ex**clud**e, in**clus**ion, **claus**trophobia pre**clud**e = "before + close" = prevent, rule out beforehand oc**clud**e = "against + close" = block off or conceal
crat crac	rule	demo**crac**y auto**crat**ic = "self + ruler" = relating to an absolute ruler or tyrant
cred creed	believe	in**cred**ible, **creed** **cred**ence = acceptance, trust **cred**ulity = readiness to believe in**cred**ulous = skeptical, unwilling to believe
dei	god	**dei**fy = "god + make" = make into a god, glorify

Root	Meaning	Examples
demo dem	people	**demo**cracy **demo**graphic = related to a population, or a segment of a population pan**dem**ic = all + people = something affecting everyone, usually a disease en**dem**ic = "in + people" = native to a population **dem**agogue = "people + lead" = leader who appeals (falsely) to the people
dict	say	pre**dict**, contra**dict**, juris**dict**ion bene**dict**ion = "good + say" = blessing vale**dict**ory = "farewell + say" = expressing a farewell (often by a speech)
duc	lead *or* pull	pro**duc**e, ab**duct**, con**duct** de**duc**e = "away + lead" = determine from general principles **duct**ile = able to be led easily (people) or to be drawn out into wire (metals) in**duct** = "in + lead" = admit as a member
dur, dure	hard *or* lasting	**dur**able, en**dure**, en**dur**ance, **dur**ation, **dur**ing **dur**ess = compulsion, restraint by force ob**dur**ate = "against + hard" = hard of heart, stubborn
equi equa	equal *or* even	**equa**tion, **equa**tor **equi**table = dealing fairly on all sides **equa**nimity = "even + spirit" = calmness under stress, balance **equi**vocate = "equal + voice" = say something open to more than one interpretation in order to mislead or to avoid commitment **equa**ble = uniform, steady, unchanging
fac fec fic fy	do *or* make	terri**fy**, puri**fy**, paci**fy**, af**fec**t, ef**fec**t, **fac**t, artifi**ci**al rare**fy** = "rare + make" = make "rare," thin, pure, less dense veri**fy** = "true + make" = confirm as true sancti**fy** = "holy + make" = make holy dei**fy** = "god + make" = make into a god, glorify bene**fic**ent = "good + do" = doing good for others male**fic**ent = "bad + do" = doing harm or evil **fac**ile = easily done or understood; lacking depth or authenticity **fac**ilitate = to make easy, help to happen **fac**titious = artificial, made-up, fake
fer	carry *or* bring	trans**fer**, of**fer**, **fer**tile, **fer**ry proli**fer**ate = "offspring + carry" = multiply in number voci**fer**ous = "voice + carry" = shouting loudly and angrily
ferv	boil	**ferv**ent = zealous, intense in feeling ef**ferv**escent = "away + boil" = being bubbly, showing exhilaration per**ferv**id = "through + boil" = over-excited, overwrought
fid	trust *or* faith	**fid**elity, con**fid**ence dif**fid**ence = "not + faith" = hesitant, lacking in self-confidence per**fid**ious = "detrimental + faith" = disloyal, treacherous
flect flex	bend	**flex**ible, re**flect**, de**flect**

Root	Meaning	Examples
flu flux fluct	flow *or* wave	**flu**id, **flu**ct**u**ate, in**flux** con**flu**ence = "together + flow" = a flowing together super**flu**ous = "over + flow" = unnecessary, wasteful melli**flu**ous = "honey + flow" = having a thick, smooth flow like honey ef**flu**vium = "out + flow" = by-product, (bad) exhalation
gen	kin *or* kind *or* birth	**gen**try = upper class **gen**tility = high social status, or conduct becoming of that status hetero**gen**eous = "different + kind" = consisting of diverse parts homo**gen**eous = "same + kind" = consisting of one substance
gno	know	a**gno**stic = "not + know" = someone who isn't sure (often about God's existence) dia**gno**sis = "through + know" = identification of (medical) causes & issues pro**gno**sticate = "before + know" = predict, foretell co**gno**scente (pl. cognoscenti) = "with + know" = expert in a subject
graph gram	write	auto**graph**, dia**gram**, **gram**mar, **graph**ic, tele**gram** mono**graph** = "one + write" = a written report or paper on a narrow subject
grade gress	step *or* go	pro**gress**, re**gress**, ag**gress**ive, con**gress** retro**grade** = "backward + go" = moving backward trans**gress**ion = "across + step" = violation of a law or rule di**gress** = "away + go" = deviate from a subject
greg	flock *or* herd	ag**greg**ate = "toward + flock" = collect or add up con**greg**ate = "together + flock" = gather together e**greg**ious = "outside + flock" = conspicuously bad, flagrant **greg**arious = sociable, companionable
her hes	stick	ad**her**e = "to + stick" = stick to co**hes**ive = "together + stick" = sticking or fitting together
jac ject	throw	e**ject**, tra**ject**ory, inter**ject**, ob**ject**ion, re**ject** ab**ject** = "away + thrown" = in a low, hopeless, depressed condition
jur	law *or* swear	**jur**y, **jur**isdiction ab**jur**e = "away + swear" = renounce or reject ad**jur**e = "toward + swear" = command, urge
leg lex lect log	word *or* speak *or* read *or* study	**lect**ure, mono**log**ue, chrono**log**ical, **lex**icon neo**log**ism = "new + word" = new word or expression eu**log**ize = "good + speak" = praise highly (often after death) eu**log**y = speech of praise
locu loqu	speak	circum**locu**tion = "around + speak" = wordiness or evasion in speech e**locu**tion = "out + speak" = art of speaking well in public **loqu**acious = very talkative

Root	Meaning	Examples
luc lus	light *or* shine *or* clear	**luc**id = clear; sane; full of light e**luc**idate = "out + shine" = make clear, explain trans**luc**ent = "through + shine" = permitting (some) passage of light pel**luc**id = "through + clear" = absolutely clear lack**lus**ter = dull, lacking brilliance
meter metr	measure	**metr**ic, alti**meter**, peri**meter**
mit miss	send	dis**miss**, e**mit**, trans**mit** **miss**ive = letter, written message re**miss** = "back + sent" = negligent, careless, lax
morph	shape	a**morph**ous = "without + shape" = shapeless meta**morph**ose = "change + shape" = transform
nom	law	auto**nom**ous = "self + law" = independent, self-contained
path	feeling	anti**path**y = "against + feeling" = strong dislike
pel puls	drive *or* push	ex**pel**, pro**pel** dis**pel** = "away + drive" = scatter, make vanish com**pel**ling = "together + drive" = convincing, forceful, attention-grabbing
phob	fear	acro**phob**ia = "high + fear" = fear of heights
phon	sound	mega**phon**e, tele**phon**e, **phon**ics homo**phon**e = "same + sound" = a word pronounced like another word caco**phon**ous = "bad + sound" = unpleasant-sounding eu**phon**y = "good + sound" = pleasing sound (usually of words)
port	carry	**port**er, trans**port**ation, im**port**, ex**port**, de**port**
pos pon	put	im**pos**e, ex**pos**e, op**pos**e, op**pon**ent, pro**pon**ent de**pos**e = "down + put" = remove a leader, or take testimony superim**pos**e = "over + on + put" = place over
prob prov	prove *or* test	**prob**e, **prov**e, im**prov**e, ap**prov**e **prob**ity = honesty, integrity re**prov**e = "back + prove" = scold, admonish, express disapproval
rog	ask *or* propose a law	inter**rog**ation, inter**rog**atory pre**rog**ative = "before + ask" = special right ar**rog**ate = "toward + ask" = claim or take (without the right) ab**rog**ate = "away + propose law" = abolish, nullify (a law or rule)
sanct	holy	**sanct**uary = holy place **sanct**ify = "holy + make" = make holy sacro**sanct** = holy, untouchable **sanct**imonious = hypocritically or falsely holy

Root	Meaning	Examples
sci	know	**sci**ence pre**sci**ent = "before + know" = knowing ahead of time, able to predict events omni**sci**ence = "all + know" = state of knowing everything
scrib script	write	**scrib**ble, **scrib**e, **script**, pre**scrib**e
sec sect	cut	**sec**tion, **sec**tor, inter**sect** bi**sect** = "two + cut" = cut in half **sect** = a subdivision or segment of a group, often of a religion
sed	sit	super**sed**e = "above + sit" = replace, transcend by being better
sequ secu sic	follow	**sequ**ence, con**sequ**ence, con**secu**tive extrin**sic** = "outside + follow" = external to something's nature intrin**sic** = "inside + follow" = internal to something's nature ob**sequ**ious = "toward + follow" = overly obedient, submissive, flattering
simil simul	similar	as**simil**ate = "toward + similar" = make or become a similar part of something **simil**itude = likeness, correspondence between two things **simul**acrum = image, semblance
son	sound	**son**ar, **son**ic **son**orous = full of rich sound dis**son**ance = "away + sound" = discord, clash of sounds
spec spect spic	look	**spec**tacle, in**spect**, retro**spect** circum**spect** = "around + look" = cautious, prudent per**spic**acious = "through + look" = able to perceive hidden truth
ten tain tend	hold *or* have *or* stretch *or* thin	re**tain**, con**tain**, ob**tain**, ex**tend** **ten**able = able to be held or maintained **ten**acity = courage, persistence, ability to hold fast abs**tain** = "away + hold" = refrain from dis**tend** = "away + stretch" = bloat, swell, expand **ten**uous = thin, weak at**ten**uate = "toward + thin" = make or become thinner or weaker
theo the	god	a**the**ist = "not + god" = someone who doesn't believe in God poly**the**ist = "many + god" = someone who believes in many gods apo**theo**sis = "away + god" = elevation to godlike status, or something that has that status
tract	drag *or* draw *or* pull	**tract**or, at**tract**, con**tract**, de**tract**, ex**tract**, re**tract** **tract**able = able to be led; obedient; easily managed abs**tract**ed = "away + drawn" = withdrawn into one's mind
trud trus	push *or* thrust	in**trud**e, ex**trud**e unob**trus**ive = "not + against + push" = not noticeable or attention-drawing abs**trus**e = "away + push" = hard to comprehend

Root	Meaning	Examples
veh vect	carry	**veh**icle, con**vec**tion, **vect**or in**vect**ive = "in + carry" = bitter criticism, denunciation **veh**ement = "carried (away) + mind" = passionate, nearly violent
ven vent	come	inter**vene**, pre**vent**, in**vent**, **event**, ad**vent**ure, **vent**ure pro**ven**ance = "forward + come" = source, or history of ownership contra**vene** = "against + come" = oppose, violate, or contradict
ver	true	**ver**ify = "true + make" = confirm as true **ver**acity = truthfulness or truth a**ver** = "toward + true" = assert, declare
vert vers	turn	re**vert**, extra**vert**, intro**vert**, ad**vers**e, inad**vert**ent, a**vers**ion, a**vert**, in**vert** **vers**atile = able to adapt easily, ready for many uses di**vert** = "away + turn" = turn aside or distract contro**vert** = "against + turn" = dispute in argument, engage in contro**vers**y
voc	voice *or* call	**voc**al, in**voc**ation equi**voc**ate = "equal + voice" = say something open to more than one interpretation in order to mislead or to avoid commitment **voc**iferous = "voice + carry" = shouting loudly and angrily
vol	will	bene**vol**ence = "good + will" = kindness, readiness to do good for others male**vol**ent = "bad + will" = wishing harm, ready to do evil

Part II: Prefixes

We must be even more careful with prefixes. Certain prefixes have relatively stable meanings (e.g., *bene-* pretty much always means "good"), but other prefixes, especially short ones that correspond to prepositions, can take on a variety of different meanings. The sense of the whole word is often unpredictable. Take a simple word: *describe* = "from + write." It is not obvious how the <u>particular</u> meaning of *describe* originates from the combination of the prefix *de-* and the root *scrib*.

Even if the meanings of the prefix and the root remain stable, the word itself may still take an unpredictable turn. For instance, *polygraph* = "many + write" = a machine that takes many medical readings at once. However, there's no reasonable way to get from that point to "lie detector," the particular "many-write" machine that provides the currently accepted sense of *polygraph*. Do not simply rely on knowing the prefix and the root separately—always learn the modern English meaning of the word itself.

Most of the examples below are repeated from the list above, so that you can see both the root and the prefix in action and reinforce the word in your memory.

Prefix	Meaning	Examples
a- an- ana-	not *or* without	**a**theist = "not + god" = someone who doesn't believe in God **a**gnostic = "not + know" = someone who isn't sure (often about God's existence) **an**archy = "not + ruler" = chaos, lack of government **ana**chronism = "not + time" = something out of place in time **a**morphous = "without + shape" = shapeless
ab- abs-	away from	**ab**normal, **ab**sent, **ab**duct **abs**tain = "away + hold" = refrain from **abs**tracted = "away + drawn" = withdrawn into one's mind **ab**jure = "away + swear" = renounce or reject **ab**ject = "away + thrown" = in a low, hopeless, depressed condition **ab**rogate = "away + propose law" = abolish, nullify (a law or rule) **abs**truse = "away + push" = hard to comprehend **abs**temious = "away + liquor" = moderate in appetite or drinking
ad- *can drop d* *and double* *next letter* ac-, ag-, as- at- etc.	to *or* toward	**ad**here = "to + stick" = stick to **ad**jure = "toward + swear" = command, urge **ac**crete = "toward + grow" = grow or pile up bit by bit **ag**gregate = "toward + flock" = collect together **as**similate = "toward + similar" = make or become a similar part of something **ar**rogate = "toward + ask" = claim or take (without the right) **at**tenuate = "toward + thin" = make or become thinner or weaker
ante-	before	**ante**cedent = "before + go" = earlier event or cause **ante**diluvian = "before + flood" = ancient, primitive
anti- ant-	against *or* opposite	**anti**biotic = "against + life" = chemical that kills bacteria **anti**pathy = "against + feeling" = strong dislike **ant**agonism = "against + struggle" = opposition, active hostility

Prefix	**Meaning**	**Examples**
auto	self	**auto**graph
		autocratic = "self + ruler" = like an absolute ruler or tyrant
		autonomous = "self + law" = independent, self-contained
be-	all the way through *(not Latin or Greek; as a native English prefix, be- often bonds to Anglo-Saxon roots)*	**be**grudge = "all the way + complain" = give unwillingly
		beguile = "all the way + trick" = deceive, divert in an attractive way
		benighted = "all the way + night" = unenlightened, in figurative darkness
		beseech = "all the way + seek" = beg, implore
		besiege = "all the way + blockade" = surround, press upon
		besmirch = "all the way + dirt" = make dirty
		beleaguered = "all the way + army camp" = pressed, troubled
bene- ben-	good	**bene**diction = "good + say" = blessing
		beneficent = "good + do" = doing good for others
		benevolence = "good + will" = kindness, readiness to do good for others
		benign = "good + birth" = favorable, gentle, harmless
bi-	two	**bi**sect = "two + cut" = cut in half
		bifurcate = "two + fork" = split into two branches
caco-	bad	**caco**phonous = "bad + sound" = unpleasant-sounding
circum-	around	**circum**ambulate = "around + walk" = walk around in a circle
		circumlocution = "around + speak" = wordiness or evasion in speech
		circumspect = "around + look" = cautious, prudent
con- com- co-	with *or* together	**con**tract, **con**tain, **con**duct
		con**greg**ate = "together + flock" = gather together
		cohesive = "together + stick" = sticking or fitting together
		compelling = "together + drive" = convincing, forceful, attention-grabbing
		confluence = "together + flow" = a flowing together
		cognoscente (pl. cognoscenti) = "with + know" = expert in a subject
contra- contro- counter-	against	**contra**dict
		contraband = "against + command" = illegal goods
		countervail = "against + worth" = compensate for, counteract, oppose
		contravene = "against + come" = oppose, violate, or contradict
		controvert = "against + turn" = dispute in argument, engage in controversy
de-	from *or* away *or* down	**de**fame, **de**odorize, **de**flect, detract
		deduce = "away + lead" = determine from general principles
		decadent = "away + fall" = in a state of decline, often self-indulgent
		derivative = "away + stream" = originating from something else; lacking originality
		depose = "down + put" = remove a leader, or take testimony
di- dia-	two through *or* across *or* between	**dia**meter, **dia**gonal
		dichotomy = division into two opposing parts
		diagnosis = "through + know" = identification of (medical) causes & issues
		diachronic = "through + time" = relating to change over time

Prefix	Meaning	Examples
dis- dys- di-	away *or* not *or* bad	**dis**allow, **dis**respect, **dis**miss, **dis**illusion, **di**vide **dis**pel = "away + drive" = scatter, make vanish **di**vert = "away + turn" = turn aside or distract **dis**sonance = "away + sound" = discord, clash of sounds **dis**tend = "away + stretch" = bloat, swell, expand **dif**fidence = "not + faith" = hesitant, lacking in self-confidence **di**gress = "away + go" = deviate from subject **dys**topia = "bad" + utopia (future/imaginary world)
duo-	two	**duo**poly = "two + sell" = condition in which there are only two sellers
en-	in	**en**demic = "in + people" = native to a population
eu-	good	**eu**logize = "good + speak" = praise highly (often after death) **eu**logy = speech of praise **eu**phony = "good + sound" = pleasing sound (usually of words)
ex- e- ef-	out *or* away *or* from	emit, **ex**pel, **ex**ceed, **ex**it, **e**ject, **ex**port ex**alt**ed = "out + high" = raised high **ex**cision = "out + cut" = act of cutting out, removing **e**locution = "out + speak" = art of speaking well in public **e**gregious = "outside + flock" = conspicuously bad, flagrant **e**lucidate = "out + shine" = make clear, explain **ef**fluvium = "out + flow" = by-product, exhalation (often bad)
extra- extr-	outside of	**extra**curricular, **exter**ior, **extr**eme **extra**polate = "outside + polish" = extend (data) to new situations, conjecture **extr**insic = "outside + follow" = external to something's nature
hetero-	other *or* different	**hetero**geneous = "different + kind" = consisting of diverse parts heterodox
homo-	same	**homo**phone = "same + sound" = a word pronounced like another word **homo**geneous = "same + kind" = consisting of one substance
hyper-	above *or* over	**hyper**sensitive, **hyper**active **hyper**bole = "above + throw" = exaggeration
hypo-	below *or* under	**hypo**allergenic, **hypo**dermic **hypo**thesis = "under" + thesis = tentative assumption to explore
in- im-	in *or* into *or* on	**in**spect, **im**port, **in**ject **in**cisive = "into + cut" = cutting to the heart of a matter, direct **in**duct = "in + lead" = admit as a member
in- im-	not	**in**credible, **im**possible, **im**penetrable, **in**evitable
infra-	below	**infra**red, **infra**structure
inter- intro-	between	**inter**national, **inter**vene, **inter**ject **inter**polate = "inside + polish" = fill in missing pieces, words, or data

Prefix	**Meaning**	**Examples**
intra- intr-	within *or* into	**intra**muscular, **intra**mural **intr**insic = "inside + follow" = internal to something's nature
magn-	big *or* great	**magn**ificent **magn**animity = "great + spirit" = nobility of spirit
mal- male-	bad	**mal**adjusted **male**volent = "bad + will" = wishing harm, ready to do evil **male**ficent = "bad + do" = doing harm or evil **mal**adroit = "bad" + adroit = lacking skill
mega- megalo-	big *or* great *or* million	**mega**phone **megalo**mania = "great + mad" = insane belief that one is all-powerful
meta-	beyond *or* change	**meta**morphose = "change + shape" = transform
micro-	small	**micro**scope, **micro**processor
mis-	bad *or* hate	**mis**apply, **mis**take, **mis**interpret **mis**anthropy = "hate + human" = hatred of humankind **mis**ogyny = "hate + women" = hatred of women
mono-	one	**mono**culture **mono**graph = "one + write" = a written report or paper on a narrow subject **mono**poly = "one + sell" = condition in which there is only one seller
multi-	many	**multi**ple, **multi**national **multi**farious = "many + places" = diverse, varied
neo-	new	**neo**logism = "new + word" = new word or expression **neo**phyte = "new + planted" = beginner, novice
non-	not	**non**sensical, **non**profit **non**descript = "not + described" = lacking distinctive qualities **non**pareil = "not + equal" = without equal **non**plus = "not + more" = perplex, baffle
ob- *can drop b* *and double* *next letter* oc-, etc.	in front of *or* against *or* toward	**ob**jection **ob**durate = "against + hard" = hard of heart, stubborn un**ob**trusive = "not + against + push" = not noticeable or attention-drawing **oc**clude = "against + close" = block off or conceal **ob**sequious = "toward + follow" = overly obedient, submissive, flattering
omni-	all	**omni**present, **omni**potent **omni**science = "all + know" = state of knowing everything
pan-	all	**pan**demic = "all + people" = something affecting everyone, usually a disease
para-	beside	**para**llel, **para**phrase

Prefix	Meaning	Examples
per-	through all the way *or* detrimental to	**per**mit **per**spicacious = "through + look" = able to perceive hidden truth **per**ambulate = "through + walk" = walk through, inspect **pel**lucid = "through + clear" = absolutely clear **per**fervid = "through + boil" = over-excited, overwrought **per**fidious = "detrimental + faith" = disloyal, treacherous
peri-	around	**peri**meter **peri**pheral = "around + carry" = on the outskirts, not central **peri**patetic = "around + walk" = moving or walking from place to place
poly-	many	**poly**technical, **poly**gon **poly**theist = "many + god" = someone who believes in many gods **poly**glot = "many + tongue" = someone who speaks many languages
pre-	before	**pre**cede **pre**cedent = "before + go" = earlier example **pre**rogative = "before + ask" = special right **pre**clude = "before + close" = prevent, rule out beforehand **pre**scient = "before + know" = knowing ahead of time, able to predict events
pro-	forward *or* before *or* for	**pro**ponent **pro**gnosticate = "before + know" = predict, foretell **pro**venance = "forward + come" = source, or history of ownership
re-	back *or* again	**re**do, **re**state, **re**flect, **re**tract, **re**ject, **re**cede **re**miss = "back + sent" = negligent, careless, lax **re**cidivism = "back + fall" = tendency to relapse to earlier behavior or crime
retro-	backward	**retro**active, **retro**spect **retro**grade = "backward + go" = moving backward
sub-	below *or* under	**sub**standard, **sub**marine **sub**ordinate = "below + order" = in a lower rank, controlled by higher ranks **sub**liminal = "below + threshold" = below the level of consciousness
super-	above *or* over	**super**natural, **super**ior **super**fluous = "over + flow" = unnecessary, wasteful **super**ficial = on the surface **super**impose = "over + on + put" = place over **super**sede = "above + sit" = replace, transcend by being better
syn-	together *or* with	**syn**thesis = "together" + thesis = combination of ideas **syn**cretism = "together + Cretan cities" = fusion of ideas and practices **syn**optic = "together + eye" = taking a comprehensive view
trans- tra-	across *or* beyond *or* through	**trans**fer, **tra**jectory, **tran**smit, **trans**portation **trans**gression = "across + step" = violation of a law or rule **trans**lucent = "through + shine" = permitting (some) passage of light

Prefix	Meaning	Examples
un-	not	**un**happy **un**obtrusive = "not + against + push" = not noticeable or attention-drawing
uni-	one	**uni**form, **uni**cycle
un-		**un**animous = "one + spirit" = in complete agreement

Part III: Suffixes

Fortunately, suffixes are much more stable in meaning than roots or prefixes. They are also limited in number, and best of all, you already know the whole set. However it is still worth looking over this list, in particular to examine how suffixes often change one part of speech into another.

Suffix	Description	Part of Speech	Made from	Examples
-able -ible	able to be X-ed	adjective	verb	think**able**, desir**able**, inconceiv**able**, frang**ible**, feas**ible**
-al -ial -ile	relating to X	adjective	noun *or* verb	triv**ial**, critic**al**, lab**ile**, duct**ile**, versat**ile**
-ance -ancy -ence -ency	state *or* process of doing X or being X	noun (abstract)	verb *or* adjective	intellig**ence**, flipp**ancy**, decad**ence**, exorbit**ance**, despond**ency**
-ant -ent	doing X	adjective *or* noun	verb	accord**ant**, account**ant**, cogniz**ant**, differ**ent**, intransig**ent**, ferv**ent**
-ar -ary	related to X	adjective	noun	sol**ar**, stell**ar**, pol**ar**
-ate (usually pronounced like *ate*) -ite	do X	verb	root	interrog**ate**, prevaric**ate**, mut**ate**, ign**ite**, exped**ite**
-ate (usually pronounced like *it*) -ite	formed by doing X *or* related to doing X	noun *or* adjective	verb	aggreg**ate**, insubordin**ate**, perquis**ite**, requis**ite**
-dom	state of being X *or* condition related to X	noun (abstract)	noun *or* adjective	free**dom**, fief**dom**, wis**dom**
-er -or	doer of X	noun (person)	verb	speak**er**, runn**er**, wander**er**
-fic	making into X *or* causing X	adjective	noun *or* adjective	horri**fic**, beati**fic**, proli**fic**, sopori**fic**
-fy -ify	make into X cause X	verb	noun *or* adjective	magni**fy**, dei**fy**, indemni**fy**, ossi**fy**, rei**fy**

Suffix	Description	Part of Speech	Made from	Examples
-ful	filled with X	adjective	noun	bounti**ful**, beauti**ful**, plenti**ful**, fret**ful**, art**ful**
-ic -iac	relating to X	adjective *or* noun	noun *or* verb	man**ic**, man**iac**, asept**ic**, bombast**ic**
-ification	process of making into X	noun (action)	noun *or* adjective	desert**ification**, ram**ification**, beaut**ification**, ed**ification**
-ine	relating to X	adjective	noun *or* verb	saturn**ine**, mar**ine**, sal**ine**, clandest**ine**
-ish	similar to X	adjective	noun *or* adjective	redd**ish**, mul**ish**, fiend**ish**, lout**ish**
-ism	system *or* characteristic of X	noun (abstract)	noun *or* adjective *or* verb	capital**ism**, social**ism**, commun**ism**, stoic**ism**, anachron**ism**, euphem**ism**
-ist -istic	characteristic of X, or a person who cspouses X	adjective *or* noun	noun *or* adjective	capital**ist**, social**ist**, commun**ist**, anachron**istic**, euphem**istic**
-ite	native or adherent of X	noun	noun *or* adjective	anchor**ite**, Ludd**ite**, sybar**ite**
-ity -ty	state or quality of being X or doing X	noun (abstract)	adjective *or* verb	polar**ity**, certain**ty**, convex**ity**, perplex**ity**
-ive -ative	tending toward the action of X	adjective	verb *or* noun	exclus**ive**, act**ive**, cohes**ive**, authorit**ative**, evas**ive**
-ize -ise	make into X	verb	adjective *or* noun	eulog**ize**, polar**ize**, scrutin**ize**, lion**ize**, advert**ise**, improv**ise**
-ization -isation	process of making into X	noun (action)	adjective	character**ization**, polar**ization**, lion**ization**, improv**isation**
-less	without X	adjective	noun	harm**less**, guile**less**, feck**less**
-ment	state or result of doing X	noun	verb	develop**ment**, judg**ment**, punish**ment**
-ory	characteristic of doing X *or* a place for doing X	adjective *or* noun	verb	refract**ory**, sav**ory**, deposit**ory**, compuls**ory**, mandat**ory**
-ous -ious -ose	characteristic of being X or doing X	adjective	verb *or* noun	carnivor**ous**, dev**ious**, numer**ous**, mellifu**ous**, menda**cious**, verb**ose**

Suffix	Description	Part of Speech	Made from	Examples
-tion -ation -ion	process *or* result of doing X	noun (action)	verb	pollu**tion**, crea**tion**, destruc**tion**
-tude	state or quality of being X	noun (abstract)	adjective	soli**tude**, vicissi**tude**, pulchri**tude**, desue**tude**

Sneak Peek at the August 2011 GRE

In mid-2011, the verbal section of the GRE will undergo some major revisions. The Analogies and Antonyms will disappear. The Sentence Completions and Reading Comprehension will remain, to be expanded and remixed in a few new ways.

In addition, the general format of the test will change. The length of the test will go from about 3.5 hours to about 4 hours. There will be two math and two verbal sections rather than one of each, and the test will be scored in one-point increments from 130–170.

For those who dislike learning vocabulary words, the changes will be something of a relief. For those who were looking forward to getting lots of points just for memorizing words, this supplement will prepare you for the shift.

Once the new test is instituted, vocabulary will still be important, but only in the context of complete sentences. You might say that ANALOGIES : GRE TEST TAKERS :: BUBONIC PLAGUE : CONTEMPORARY SOCIETY. That is, you'll no longer have to worry about esoteric vocabulary words standing alone.

New Verbal Problem Formats in Brief:

> Reading Comprehension—While this question type tests the same skills as before, some of the questions will look quite strange, such as those that ask you to select "one or more" answer choices. Some questions will ask you to highlight the sentence in a passage that meets a certain description.

> Text Completion—"Sentence Completions" are now "Text Completions." From this, you might correctly infer that the text can now be more than one sentence long. It can also contain 1, 2, or 3 blanks that you will be asked to fill in with the answer choices. When there are 2 or 3 blanks, you will select the words or phrases to fill in each blank *independently* of one another. Fortunately, the number of choices in these problems has been reduced from five to three for each blank.

> Sentence Equivalence—These questions look a lot like Sentence Completions, except that there are six answers, and TWO of them are correct. If you guessed that that would make life easier since the two choices you pick would have to be synonyms, you'd be right!

We're about to discuss strategies for Text Completion and Sentence Equivalence. But overall, don't worry! The same core skills are being tested, and most of the material you've put time into studying for the current GRE will still be useful for the August 2011 GRE. Also, as you're about to see, many of these problem types aren't as different as they might seem.

Finally, don't worry about whether these new problem types are "harder" or "easier." You're being judged against other students, all of whom are in the same boat. So if the new formats are harder, they're harder for other test takers as well; likewise if they're easier. The upcoming strategies and problem sets will put you ahead of the game!

Text Completion Questions

Text Completions are the new, souped-up Sentence Completions. They can consist of 1–5 sentences with 1–3 blanks. When Text Completions have two or three blanks, you will select those blanks independently. There is no partial credit; you must make every selection correctly.

Because this makes things a bit harder, the GRE has kindly reduced the number of possible choices per blank from five to three. Here is an old two-blank Sentence Completion, as it would appear on the new GRE:

Current Format:

> Leaders are not always expected to _____ the same rules as are those they lead; leaders are often looked up to for a surety and presumption that would be viewed as _____ in most others.
>
> A. obey ... avarice
>
> B. proscribe ... insalubriousness
>
> C. decree ... anachronism
>
> D. conform to ... hubris
>
> E. follow ... eminence

New August 2011 Format:

> Directions: For each blank select one entry from the corresponding column of choices. Fill all blanks in the way that best completes the text.
>
> Leaders are not always expected to _____ the same rules as are those they lead; leaders are often looked up to for a surety and presumption that would be viewed as _____ in most others.
>
> | Blank (1) | Blank (2) |
> |-----------|-----------|
> | decree | hubris |
> | proscribe | avarice |
> | conform to | anachronism |

(The GRE hasn't yet specified exactly *how* you will physically select your answer, but whether you are highlighting or clicking a selection button, we're sure they'll make it perfectly obvious.)

Solution:

In the first blank, we need a word similar to "follow." In the second blank, we need a word similar to "arrogant." Only choice D works in the current format; in the new format, the answer is still "conform to" and "hubris," but you'll make the two choices separately.

Note that in the "Current Format" question, if you knew that you needed a word in the second blank that meant something like "arrogant," and you knew that "hubris" was the only word in the second column with the correct meaning, you could pick correct answer choice D without even considering the first word in each pair. In the new format, this strategy is no longer available to us.

Also note that, in the "Current Format" question, "obey," "conform to," and "follow" mean basically the same thing. On the new GRE, this can't happen: since you select each word independently, no two choices can be synonyms (otherwise, there would be two correct answers).

Strategy Tip: As on the current GRE, do NOT look at the answer choices until you've decided for yourself, based on textual clues actually written in the sentence, what kind of word needs to go in each blank. Only then should you look at the choices and eliminate those that are not matches.

Let's try an example with three blanks.

Directions: For each blank select one entry from the corresponding column of choices. Fill all blanks in the way that best completes the text.

For Kant, the fact of having a right and having the _____ to enforce it via coercion cannot be separated, and he asserts that this marriage of rights and coercion is compatible with the freedom of everyone. This is not at all peculiar from the standpoint of modern political thought—what good is a right if its violation triggers no enforcement (be it punishment or _____)? The necessity of coercion is not at all in conflict with the freedom of everyone, because this coercion only comes into play when someone has _____ someone else.

Blank (1)	Blank (2)	Blank (3)
technique	amortization	questioned the hypothesis of
license	reward	violated the rights of
prohibition	restitution	granted civil liberties to

Solution:

In the first sentence, use the clue "he asserts that this marriage of rights and coercion is compatible with the freedom of everyone" to help fill in the first blank. Kant believes that "coercion" is "married to" rights and is compatible with freedom for all. So we want something in the first blank like "right" or "power." Kant believes that rights are meaningless without enforcement. Only the choice "license" can work (while a "license" can be physical, like a driver's license, "license" can also mean "right").

The second blank is part of the phrase "punishment or _____," which we are told is the "enforcement" resulting from the violation of a right. So the blank should be something, other than punishment, that constitutes enforcement against someone who violates a right. (More simply, it should be something bad!) Only "restitution" works. Restitution is compensating the victim in some way (perhaps monetarily or by returning stolen goods).

In the final sentence, "coercion only comes into play when someone has _____ someone else." Throughout the text, "coercion" means enforcement against someone who has violated the rights of someone else. The meaning is the same here. The answer is "violated the rights of."

The complete and correct answer is this combination:

Blank (1)	Blank (2)	Blank (3)
license	restitution	violated the rights of

In theory, there are $3 \times 3 \times 3 = 27$ possible ways to answer a 3-blank Text Completion—and only one of those 27 ways is correct. The guessing odds will go down, but don't be intimidated. Just follow the basic process: come up with your own filler for each blank, and match to the answer choices.

Strategy Tip: As on the current GRE, do NOT "write your own story." The GRE cannot give you a blank without also giving you a clue, physically written down in the passage, telling you what kind of word or phrase MUST go in that blank. Find that clue. You should be able to give textual evidence for each answer choice you select.

Sentence Equivalence Questions

In this question type, you are given one sentence with a single blank. There are six answer choices, and you are asked to pick TWO choices that fit the blank and are alike in meaning.

Of the new question types, this one depends the most on vocabulary and also yields the most to strategy.

No partial credit is given on Sentence Equivalence; both correct answers must be selected. When you pick two of six choices, there are 15 possible combinations of choices, and only one is correct. However, this is not nearly as daunting as it sounds.

Think of it this way—if you have six choices, but the two correct ones must be "similar in meaning," then you have, at most, three possible PAIRS of choices. Maybe fewer, since not all choices are guaranteed to have a "partner." If you can match up the "pairs," you can seriously narrow down your options.

Here is a sample set of answer choices:

> A. tractable
> B. taciturn
> C. arbitrary
> D. tantamount
> E. reticent
> F. amenable

We haven't even given you the question here, because we want to point out how much you can do with the choices alone, if you have studied vocabulary sufficiently.

TRACTABLE and AMENABLE are synonyms (tractable, amenable people will do whatever you want them to do). TACITURN and RETICENT are synonyms (both mean "not talkative"). ARBITRARY (based on one's own will) and TANTAMOUT (equivalent) are not similar in meaning and therefore cannot be a pair. Therefore, the ONLY possible answers are {A, F} and {B, E}. We have improved our chances from 1 in 15 to a 50/50 shot without even reading the question!

Of course, in approaching a Sentence Equivalence, we do want to analyze the sentence the same way we would with a Text Completion—read for a textual clue that tells you what type of word MUST go in the blank. Then look for a matching pair.

Strategy Tip: If you're sure that a word in the choices does NOT have a partner, cross it out! For instance, if A and C are partners, and E and F are partners, and you're sure B and D are not each other's partners, cross out B and D completely. They cannot be the answer together, nor can either one be part of the answer.

The sentence for the answer choice above could read,

> Though the dinner guests were quite _____ , the hostess did her best to keep the conversation active and engaging.

Thus, B and E are the best choices.

Let's try an example.

> While athletes usually expect to achieve their greatest feats in their teens or twenties, opera singers don't reach the _____ of their vocal powers until middle age.

    A. harmony

    B. zenith

    C. acme

    D. terminus

    E. nadir

    F. cessation

Solution:

Let's run through two approaches.

Approach #1: Without looking at the choices, hunt through the sentence for a clue about what kind of word goes in the blank. We are comparing the "greatest feats" of athletes to something similar about opera singers. Fill in the blank in your own words with something like "peak." Now go to the choices. Say you knew that ZENITH was correct, but you weren't sure about the other choice. Write this on your paper:

ZENITH
A
C
D
E
F

(That is, put the word you're trying to "match" up top and write the letter of each answer choice except the one written at top).

Now cross off any options that definitely DON'T mean zenith or peak. You might end up with something like this:

ZENITH
~~A~~
C
~~D~~
E
~~F~~

The test-taker above has crossed off three choices, leaving a guess between {B, C} and {B, D}. The correct answer is {B, C}.

Approach #2: Those with strong vocabularies might go straight to the choices to make pairs. ZENITH and ACME are synonyms, meaning "high point, peak." TERMINUS and CESSATION are synonyms, meaning "end." NADIR is a low point and HARMONY is present here as a trap answer reminding us of opera singers. *Cross off A and E, since they do not have partners.* Then, go back to the sentence, knowing that your only options are a pair meaning "peak" and a pair meaning "end."

Again, the answer is {B, C}.

Problem Set

Text Completion and Sentence Equivalence Practice

The following is a short practice set composed of two of the three new problem types. Note that, on the real exam, these new problem types will be mixed in with "regular" Reading Comprehension questions (select one choice out of five), new Reading Comprehension questions, and "regular" one-blank Sentence Completions (now called Text Completions, but the one-blank questions will have five choices, just as on the current GRE).

1. A parliament can become _____, unable to get much of anything done, when its members devolve into _____, adhering to group allegiances with little regard for the exigencies of actual government.

Blank (1)	Blank (2)
venomous	duplicity
stagnant	recidivism
apollonian	factionalism

2. Because Mariel was the _____ of the office, her sudden absence meant that interdepartmental projects floundered without their usual liaison among the company's divisions.

    A. ascetic

    B. hub

    C. lackey

    D. linchpin

    E. sybarite

    F. cog

3. Despite constant _____ and even bribery, he wouldn't agree to do something that was against his conscience.

    A. jocularity

    B. wheedling

    C. mirthfulness

    D. tractability

    E. inveigling

    F. complaisance

4. Bentham's Panopticon was a prison constructed in such a way that one guard can see any of the prisoners from a single hub. Not knowing if he or she is being watched at any given moment, each prisoner cannot help but _____ his or her own behavior as though he or she were, in fact, being watched. Of course, the Panopticon was a metaphor for society, in which citizens are _____ by a _____ authority.

Blank (1)	Blank (2)	Blank (3)
reduce	imprisoned	central
chastise	punished	judicial
police	monitored	pernicious

5. Progeria is an extremely rare genetic condition causing those affected to age very _____, causing young children to look like very small elderly people, complete with balding and wrinkles. Scientists are interested in the study of progeria because they suspect it might yield clues about the normal aging process; however, some critics are _____ studying a genetic rarity will produce results _____ to humans at large.

Blank (1)	Blank (2)	Blank (3)
tacitly	convinced that the benefits of	interesting
randomly	incredulous that data gleaned from	applicable
rapidly	determined to prove that	inept

6. Jorge called in two assistants to help him _____ the pile of applications down to the few strongest ones, which would then be _____ by a committee.

Blank (1)	Blank (2)
transform	vetted
winnow	convoked
apprise	fomented

7. Before arriving in a war-torn area, aid workers can often only _____ about the conditions on the ground, later taking in the situation when they arrive and either confirming or modifying their original expectations.

A. hypothesize

B. imply

C. declaim

D. theorize

E. extrapolate

F. infer

the new standard

Solutions

Text Completion and Sentence Equivalence Practice

1. A parliament can become _____, unable to get much of anything done, when its members devolve into _____, adhering to group allegiances with little regard for the exigencies of actual government.

Blank (1)	Blank (2)
venomous	duplicity
stagnant	recidivism
apollonian	factionalism

Answer: {**stagnant, factionalism**}

The first blank is followed by a modifier set off by commas, "unable to get much of anything done." Thus, the meaning of the first word should be similar to "unable to get much of anything done." Similarly, the second blank is also followed by a modifier set off by commas, "adhering to group allegiances…." Thus, the word in the blank should express the meaning of sticking to a group membership despite other considerations; *factionalism* means just that.

2. Because Mariel was the _____ of the office, her sudden absence meant that interdepartmental projects floundered without their usual liaison among the company's divisions.

    A. ascetic

    B. hub

    C. lackey

    D. linchpin

    E. sybarite

    F. cog

Answer: {**B, D**}

The second part of the sentence tells us that "interdepartmental projects floundered without their usual liaison"—that is, Mariel was the liaison among the company's divisions. Thus, she was the *hub* or *linchpin*, a center around which things revolve, or something that holds complicated elements together. (Note that C and F are similar to each other, but A and E are each without a "partner" and thus cannot be correct).

3. Despite constant _____ and even bribery, he wouldn't agree to do something that was against his conscience.

    A. jocularity

    B. wheedling

    C. mirthfulness

    D. tractability

    E. inveigling

    F. complaisance

Answer: {**B, E**}

The sentence contains two clues. First, the word in the blank should be similar to but less extreme than "bribery." Second, we know that "despite" the word in first blank, the person in question wouldn't do something that was against his conscience; therefore the word in the blank should be something that might lead a person to go against his conscience. *Wheedling* and *inveigling* both meet this description. (Note that A and C make a pair here, as do D and F).

4. Bentham's Panopticon was a prison constructed in such a way that one guard can see any of the prisoners from a single hub. Not knowing if he or she is being watched at any given moment, each prisoner cannot help but _____ his or her own behavior as though he or she were, in fact, being watched. Of course, the Panopticon was a metaphor for society, in which citizens are _____ by a _____ authority.

Blank (1)	Blank (2)	Blank (3)
reduce	imprisoned	central
chastise	punished	judicial
police	monitored	pernicious

Answer: {**police, monitored, central**}

Since the prisoner cannot know if he or she is being watched, he or she acts as though he or she is being watched. Thus, each prisoner cannot help but *police* his or her own behavior. The final sentence mirrors the meaning of the first. In the first sentence, it is explained that, in the Panopticon, prisoners are *watched* by a guard *from a central hub*. In the last sentence, we learn that the Panopticon was a metaphor for society; thus, citizens are *monitored* by a *central* authority.

5. Progeria is an extremely rare genetic condition causing those affected to age very _____, causing young children to look like very small elderly people, complete with balding and wrinkles. Scientists are interested in the study of progeria because they suspect it might yield clues about the normal aging process; however, some critics are _____ studying a genetic rarity will produce results _____ to humans at large.

Blank (1)	Blank (2)	Blank (3)
tacitly	convinced that the benefits of	interesting
randomly	incredulous that data gleaned from	applicable
rapidly	determined to prove that	inept

Answer: {**rapidly, incredulous that data gleaned from, applicable**}

If young children "look like very small elderly people," they must be aging *rapidly.* In the next sentence, the "however" tells us that the second part of the sentence should be opposite in meaning to the first (we also have another clue with the word "critics"—the critics should have an opposite view to the scientists). Since scientists think that the study of progeria *might yield clues about the normal aging process,* the critics of those scientists are disbelieving, or *incredulous that data gleaned from* such studies will produce results *applicable* to humans at large—that is, to those subject to the "normal aging process."

6. Jorge called in two assistants to help him _____ the pile of applications down to the few strongest ones, which would then be _____ by a committee.

Blank (1)	Blank (2)
transform	vetted
winnow	convoked
apprise	fomented

Answer: {**winnow, vetted**}

Jorge wants to go from a "pile" of applications to "the few strongest ones." To *winnow* is to separate out the bad from the good. After this perhaps cursory look by Jorge and the assistants, the strongest applications would be looked at more closely—that is, vetted—by a committee.

7. Before arriving in a war-torn area, aid workers can often only _____ about the conditions on the ground, later taking in the situation when they arrive and either confirming or modifying their original expectations.

    A. hypothesize

    B. imply

    C. declaim

    D. theorize

    E. extrapolate

    F. infer

Answer: {**A, D**}

After arriving, the workers take in the situation and confirm or modify their original expectations. However, before they arrive, they can "only" perform the action in the blank. The action in the blank must be something lesser than and preliminary to gaining real information and using it to make judgments. This is a match for *hypothesize* and *theorize*. *Infer* is a close miss: you *infer from* conditions *that* something is true, but you don't *infer about* conditions or anything else. Likewise, you can *extrapolate from* data to make a prediction, but you don't *extrapolate about* something. Pay attention to the precise usage of words in the answer choices. *Declaim* and *imply* have no partners, so you can eliminate those choices if you are working backward.

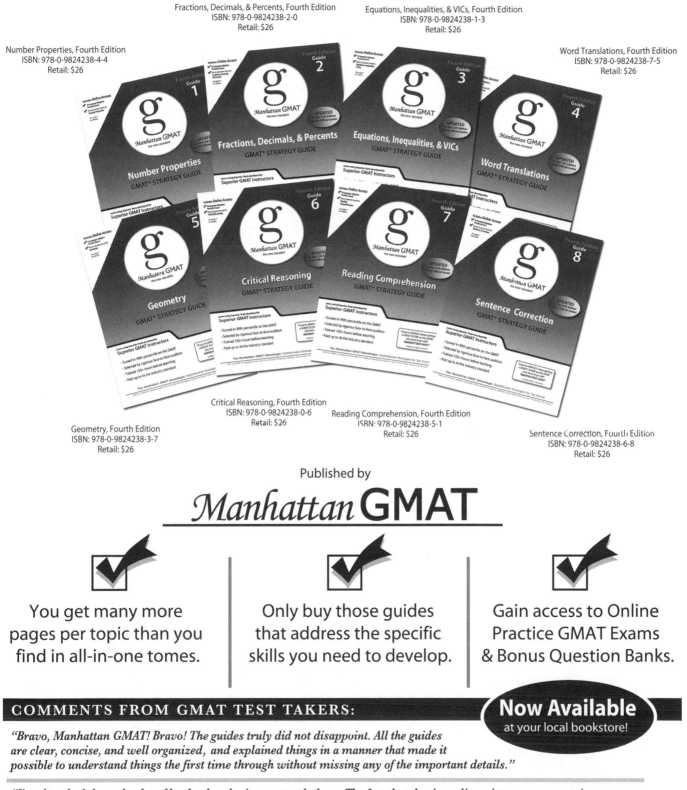